MW00996805

Read All About It

Starter

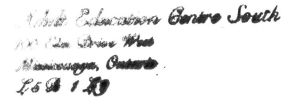

Susan Iannuzzi
Renée Weiss

Series Editor: Lori Howard

OXFORD
UNIVERSITY PRESS

Oxford University Press
98 Madison Avenue
New York, NY 10016 USA

Great Clarendon Street
Oxford OX2 6DP England

Oxford New York
Auckland Bangkok Buenos Aires Cape Town Chennai
Dar es Salaam Delhi Hong Kong Istanbul Karachi
Kolkata Kuala Lumpur Madrid Melbourne Mexico City
Mumbai Nairobi São Paulo Shanghai Taipei Tokyo
Toronto

OXFORD is a trademark of Oxford University Press

ISBN 0-19-438654-6

Copyright © 2005 Oxford University Press

Cataloging-in-Publication data is available.

No unauthorized photocopying.

All rights reserved. No part of this publication may be
reproduced, stored in a retrieval system, or transmitted, in any
form or by any means, electronic, mechanical, photocopying,
recording, or otherwise, without the prior written permission
of Oxford University Press.

This book is sold subject to the condition that it shall not, by
way of trade or otherwise, be lent, resold, hired out, or
otherwise circulated without the publisher's prior consent in
any form of binding or cover other than that in which it is
published and without a similar condition including this
condition being imposed on the subsequent purchaser.

Executive Publisher: Janet Aitchison
Editor: Margaret Brooks
Art Director: Lynn Luchetti
Production Manager: Shanta Persaud
Production Controller: Eve Wong

Printing (last digit): 10 9 8 7 6 5 4 3 2 1

Printed in Hong Kong

Acknowledgments
Illustrations and realia by:
Barbara Bastian, 33, 39, 44, 64; Ken Batelman, 8
(thermometer), 24, 61; Mary Chandler, 29, 47; Steve
Chorney/Mendola, 18, 45; Matt Collins, 7; Mona Daly/Mendola,
30 (icons), 75, 76; Paul Hampson, 15, 65; Mike Hortens, 8
(map), 54, 68; Jon Keegan, 1, 30 (supermarket); Don
Morrison/Anita Grien, 27, 48, 59

The publishers would like to thank the following for their
permission to reproduce photographs:
Tom Bean, 55 (Standin' on the Corner Park, Winslow, AZ);
Craig E. Biertempfel, 68 (Pennsylvania Macaroni Company
store); Gregorio Binuya, 42 (Cynthia Rowley); Comstock, 67
(family-run restaurant); Corbis, 6 (Groundhog Day), 24 (yurt),
72 (woman/laundry); Jim Corwin/Indexstock Imagery,
3 (moon); Dr. John Crossley, 10 (redwoods), 54 (deserted
town); R. Dias/Robertstock, 7 (rainy day); Digital Vision
Photography, 8 (Asian father & son), 62 (driving test); Kevin
Dodge, 21 (Hispanic male), 51 (medical consultation), 73
(African-American woman); Britt Erslandson/Stone/Getty
Images, 17 (multi-generational family); Paul Franklin, 24
(lakeside yurt); Joe Giardina, 58 (block party); John Gilmore,
23 (treehouse) Peter Griffith/Masterfile, 21 (Asian female);
Grant Heilman, 3 (cows); ImageSource, 21 (man with glasses);
M. Mayer/ZEFA, 67 (bakers); Michael McGovern/Nonstock,
14 (subway train); Jean-Pierre Muller/AFP, 41 (runway model);
National Route 66 Organization, 55 (Midpoint sign, Adrian,
TX); Dr. Susan Osborne, 46 (Dr. Osborne); Oxford University
Press, 6 (groundhog); Chuck Pefley, 53 (crowds); Photodisc,
79 (men exercising), 41 (woman and dog); Photofusion
Library, 72 (daycare); Photonica/Alamy, 41 (businesspeople);
Punchstock/Thinkstock, 2 (red sky); Rubberball, 67
(parent/computer); Dave L. Ryan, 53 (small town); Hazel
Schmeiser/Unicorn Photos, 27 (houseboat); SnowWorld.com,
76 (Snowdome); Inga Spence, 10 (logger); Veer/Digital Vision
Photography, 35 (family-style restaurant); Shaun Walker/Otter
Media.com, 11 (Julia Hill on phone, Julia Hill climbing in tree);
Michael Weaver/Alamy, 2 (horses); Renee Weiss, 36 (interior &
exterior of Nat's Restaurant); Kurt Wittman/Omni Photo, 58
(community garden)

Special thanks to:
Julia Hill and the Circle of Life, 11; Nat's Early Bite Coffee
Shop, 36; Dr. Susan Osborne of the Barter Clinic, 48; Bill
Sunseri and The Pennsylvania Macaroni Company, 69

The authors and publishers extend their thanks to the
following English Language Teaching professionals for their
support and feedback during the development of this book:
Amy Cooper, Jill Gluck, Nancy Hampson, Maria Miranda, Jean
Rose, Kristin Sherman, Laura Webber

TO THE TEACHER

Welcome to the *Read All About It* series.

Read All About It Starter is a collection of engaging articles and stories for adult and young adult students of English as a Second or Foreign Language at a beginning level.

Each of the twelve thematic units in this book contains two high-interest readings based on authentic materials, including news stories, magazine articles, biographies, brochures, web pages, and advertisements. The readings and activities in each unit focus on one topic such as housing, food, or clothing. This gives students the opportunity to read, listen, speak, and write about one topic in depth and to reinforce and expand their knowledge of related vocabulary. A wide variety of pre-reading, reading, and post-reading activities gives students numerous opportunities to develop cultural awareness as well as problem solving and critical thinking skills. Students will also build reading fluency through the practice of skills such as predicting, scanning, guessing meaning from context, and comprehension.

Read All About It Starter is interactive. Students are encouraged to interact with the text by using their knowledge and experience to help them understand the readings. Students can also interact with each other as they complete the many thought provoking pair and group activities that accompany the readings.

Read All About It Starter is designed to be flexible and adaptable to the needs of classes and individual students. It can be used as a core reader, as a reading supplement, or for independent study. An accompanying CD includes recordings of all the readings. Students who are also using *The Basic Oxford Picture Dictionary* will find that *Read All About It Starter* helps bring the *Dictionary* vocabulary to life. Each unit in *Read All About It Starter* focuses on the same topic and vocabulary as the corresponding unit in *The Basic Oxford Picture Dictionary* and incorporates vocabulary from other units as well.

Students who use *Read All About It Starter* will gain confidence in their reading ability and learn that they can understand what they read without knowing every word. The strategies they learn will help them to enjoy reading and encourage them to read more.

Tour of a Unit

TALK ABOUT IT, usually led by the teacher, is aimed at introducing the topic, motivating the students, and encouraging them to share their prior knowledge about it. The open-ended activities presented in this section allow students of varying abilities to participate and benefit. They can share their personal experiences through guided discussions with classmates.

READ ABOUT IT includes pre-reading, reading, and post-reading activities. Although some activities (see, for example, *Talk more about it*) direct students to work in pairs or small groups, most of the activities can be done individually.

Before You Read asks students to gather more specific information about the upcoming passage just as competent readers do. Students look at illustrations or photos that accompany the reading, as well as the title and headings, and make predictions about the reading. New vocabulary is introduced in context and, in many cases, is evident in the captions of the pictures. *Before You Read* can be teacher-led or done individually and then discussed with the whole group.

While You Read focuses students on the reading and asks them to reflect on their pre-reading predictions as they read silently. Students are not expected to understand every word; they should be encouraged to read for the general meaning and to use context clues and their background knowledge to aid comprehension. Activities include:

▶ ***What did you read?*** Students are asked to identify the main idea of the reading.

▶ ***Read again*** provides students with a second opportunity to read the whole passage or parts of the passage silently, focusing on a set of comprehension questions.

▶ ***Show you understand*** asks students to demonstrate their comprehension of the passage in a variety of ways such as using vocabulary in context, categorizing and sequencing ideas.

▶ **Talk more about it** invites students to relate the material they have read to their experience and knowledge and use it to discuss their own ideas. Most students at this level will begin by offering short answers, but as they become accustomed to the activity, they may have more to contribute.

After You Read helps students to further develop their vocabulary and reading skills. Students practice writing, which supports and reinforces the reading. Depending on the time available, these activities can be either done in class or assigned for homework.

READ MORE ABOUT IT offers an opportunity for students to read further about the same topic. Shorter than READ ABOUT IT, it is similar in format and includes many of the same kinds of activities.

Special Features

Teacher's Notes

Teacher's Notes include general information about using this book, specific information about each unit, and suggested extension activities.

Answer Key

A removable Answer Key is available for individuals to check their work. However, when students are working in pairs or small groups, they should be encouraged to check their answers with each other to maximize peer interaction. This flexibility makes *Read All About It Starter* useful in classroom, laboratory, and home settings alike.

Word List

A unit-by-unit word list provides *Basic Oxford Picture Dictionary* page references for vocabulary used in this book, so that students who have the *Dictionary* can use it for support. Teachers can also use the list to determine which words in the readings appear in the *Dictionary*.

Remember the Words

A personal vocabulary diary helps students learn new words of their choice.

We hope you and your students enjoy *Read All About It Starter*, and we welcome your comments and ideas.

Write to us at:
Oxford University Press
English Language Teaching Division
198 Madison Avenue
New York, New York 10016
Susan Iannuzzi
Renee Weiss
Lori Howard (Series Editor)

Author's Acknowledgments

We would like to thank these people for their help and support in this project:

Janet Aitchison, Executive Publisher, for her continued dedication and vision for *The Oxford Picture Dictionary Program*;

Meg Brooks, Editor, for bringing both knowledge and a keen eye to this project and for her steadfast care in keeping the manuscript in excellent hands from start to finish;

Lori Howard, Series Editor, for providing the "heart and soul" that is *Read All About It*;

Jayme Adelson-Goldstein, for lifelong professional and personal friendship;

From Renee Weiss:

Sincere thanks to the entire Oxford Sales and Marketing team for supporting all my professional endeavors and allowing me to wear many "hats," to owner Victor Carlos, family, and loyal patrons of Nat's Early Bite Coffee Shop for their warm cooperation. Good food and friendship served all day!

and, finally, loving gratitude to husband Malcolm Loeb and daughter Sophie, who give me strength and inspiration as I write, late into the night.

From Susan Iannuzzi:

Susan would like to thank Atef Ramzy for his keen insight and suggestions. Also, thanks are due to my husband, Emeil Shenouda, and our daughter, Mira, for their constant love and indulgence of my need to write.

Dedication

We lovingly dedicate this book to our friend and colleague Norma Shapiro, who has enriched our lives with her wisdom, humor and courage. In remembrance, we will continue to teach her lessons—of friendship, love, family, and community.

CONTENTS

TALK ABOUT IT

A. Look at the weather on the TV and outside in the garden. Is it the same or different? Mark (✗) the correct boxes in the chart.

The weather outside	TV weather report	
	SAME	DIFFERENT
It's windy.		✗
It's cloudy.		
It's raining.		
It's 68 degrees.		

B. Think about these questions. Then ask and answer the questions with a partner.

1. How is the weather today?
2. What is the temperature today?
3. What kind of weather do you like?

READ ABOUT IT

A red sky at night

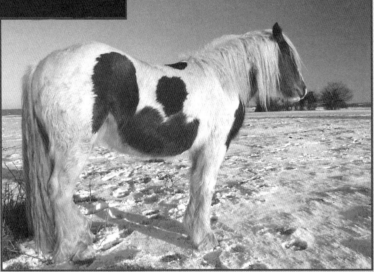

Horse with a heavy winter coat

Before You Read

Look at the pictures. Look at the title of the reading. Guess the answer to the question. Circle *a* or *b*.

What is this reading about?

a. the weather   **b.** farm animals

Read this magazine article. Think about your guess while you read.

How's the Weather?

A circle around the moon

Everybody thinks about it. Everybody talks about it. What is it? It's the weather! Some people watch the weather report on television. Some people listen to the weather report on the radio. Other people use old ideas and sayings to learn about the weather.

These people look at the sky in the evening. They look for a white circle around the moon. This means snow is coming tomorrow. They count the stars around the moon. Four stars means snow is coming in four days!

The cows are sleeping more.

Fishermen say, "A red sky at night means a sunny day and blue skies tomorrow. A red sky in the morning means gray, cloudy skies and rain today." Some Native Americans say, "A red moon means rainy weather tomorrow."

Farmers look at their animals in the fall. The horses have heavy coats. The cows are sleeping more. The farmers say, "The weather is changing. A cold winter is coming."

What's the weather for tomorrow? Look around. Look at the sky—the sun, the moon, and the stars. Look at the animals. Then you'll know.

▶ *What did you read?*

What is the reading about? Circle the best answer.

a. weather reports on television   **b.** old ideas and sayings about the weather

▶ *Read again*

What do the items in column A tell you about the weather? Match column A with column B. Write the correct letter in the blank.

	A		B
_c_	**1.** a red sky at night	**a.**	a cold winter
___	**2.** four stars around the moon	**b.**	snow tomorrow
___	**3.** a red sky in the morning	**c.**	a blue sky tomorrow
___	**4.** horses with heavy coats	**d.**	snow in four days
___	**5.** a circle around the moon	**e.**	a rainy day today

▶ *Show you understand*

Find more words in the reading for these categories. Write them in the chart.

COLORS	TIMES OF DAY	THINGS IN THE SKY	WEATHER
white	evening	moon	snow

▶ *Talk more about it*

Think about these questions. Then talk about your ideas with a partner.

> **1.** How do you learn about the weather?
>
> **2.** What sayings about the weather do you know? Are these sayings true?

After You Read

▶ *Words, words, words*

Copy the sentences. Change the underlined words. Use the words in the box.

cloudy	morning	tomorrow	snow	stars

1. What's the weather for <u>today</u>?   *What's the weather for tomorrow?*

2. The weather report says, "<u>Rain</u> today."   _____

3. I like <u>sunny</u> weather.   _____

4. Look at the <u>moon</u> in the sky.   _____

5. The sky is red in the <u>evening</u>.   _____

▶ *Puzzle: A secret word*

Unscramble these words from the reading. Write the letters in the boxes.

RDE ▢◯▢

TDYOA ▢▢▢◯▢

MGIONRN ▢▢◯▢▢▢▢

BUEL ▢▢▢◯

TROMOWOR ▢▢▢▢▢▢▢◯

NTGHI ▢▢▢▢◯

WEIHT ▢◯▢▢▢

Write the letters in the circles here.

__ __ __ __ __ __ __

Now unscramble the secret word. Use it to complete this sentence.

The _____ is always changing.

The groundhog looks out of its hole.

Groundhog Day

Before You Read

Look at the pictures. Look at the title of the reading. Guess the answers to the questions. Circle *a* or *b*.

1. Where does the groundhog sleep?

    a. in a tree   **b.** under the ground

2. The groundhog wakes up. What does it see?

    a. its shadow   **b.** a cloudy day

Read this textbook article. Think about your guesses while you read.

The Groundhog Weather Report

In the United States, February 2 is Groundhog Day. In the north, the weather is cold in the winter. In some places, the temperature is below freezing. There is snow on the ground. Many people don't like cold weather. They like warm weather. They ask, "When is spring coming?" Do groundhogs know the answer? Some people say, *Yes*!

Groundhogs are small brown animals. They live in holes under the ground. Groundhogs are active in the summer. They run around. They eat green plants. They enjoy the warm summer days. But in the fall, in November and December, the weather gets cold. Then the groundhogs go into their holes. They sleep in their holes all winter.

On February 2, people watch for the "Groundhog Weather Report." What does the groundhog do? The groundhog wakes up early in the morning. It leaves its hole in the ground and goes outside. Sometimes it's a sunny day. Then the groundhog sees its shadow. It goes back into its hole. Oh, no! That means six more weeks of winter. But sometimes the weather on Groundhog Day is cloudy. The groundhog doesn't see its shadow. Spring is near!

The groundhog is sleeping.

The groundhog sees its shadow.

Six more weeks of winter!

▶ *Read again*

Complete these sentences. Circle *a* or *b*.

1. Groundhog Day is in _____.   **a.** February   **b.** November

2. Many people don't like _____ weather.   **a.** warm   **b.** cold

3. The groundhog is a small _____ animal.   **a.** brown   **b.** black

4. Groundhogs sleep all _____.   **a.** summer   **b.** winter

5. It's sunny. Six more _____ of winter!   **a.** days   **b.** weeks

▶ *Write*

Look at the picture. Complete the weather report for the day in the picture.

Good morning. The weather
today is _____
and _____. The
temperature is _____.
It's very _____.

 Turn to *Remember the Words*, page 104.

TALK ABOUT IT

A. Work with a partner. Look at a typical day for Joseph and his son J.J. Answer the questions in the chart below. Mark (✗) the correct boxes.

```
Joseph
4:30 a.m. - get up
5:00 a.m. - eat breakfast
6:00 a.m. - open the store
12:30 p.m.- J.J. arrives at store
5:45 p.m. - eat dinner
6:45 p.m. - play soccer-Lincoln Park
9:00 p.m. - go to bed

J.J.
10:00 a.m.- get up
12:30 p.m.- start work at store
5:00 p.m. - come home
5:45 p.m. - eat dinner
7:00 p.m. - go to class at the university,
10:00 p.m.- come home/study
1:00 a.m. - go to sleep
```

Who...	JOSEPH	J.J.
gets up at 10 a.m.?		✗
works at the store in the morning?		
eats dinner at 5:45?		
goes to the university in the evening?		
goes to bed early?		

What do Joseph and J.J. do together?

B. Think about these questions. Then ask and answer the questions with your partner.

> **1.** What activities do you do every day?
>
> **2.** What do you and your family or friends do together?

A California redwood tree

A lumber worker cuts down a tree.

Before You Read

Look at the pictures. Look at the title of the reading. Guess the answers to the questions. Circle *a* or *b*.

1. Where is Julia living?

   a. near a tree   **b.** in a tree

2. What does Julia do every day?

   a. visits friends   **b.** reads letters

Read this magazine article. Think about your guesses while you read.

Life Above Ground

Welcome to the home of Julia "Butterfly" Hill! Julia is a young woman. She is 25 years old. It is 1997, and she is living in a large California redwood tree. This tree is over 600 years old.

Julia wants to save trees like this one. A lumber company wants to cut them down. But the company can't cut down this tree. Julia is living in it!

What does Julia do every day? She gets up early. The mornings are cold, so she gets dressed fast. She combs her hair and washes her face. Then she cooks breakfast.

In the morning, Julia reads her mail. She gets a lot of letters every week. In the afternoon, she exercises. She climbs around in the tall tree. After that, she talks to many people on her cell phone. Many people want to learn about her ideas. Friends come. They bring fresh water, food, and clothes. Julia goes to sleep at 9:00 p.m.

Julia lives in the tree for 738 days. Life in the tree is difficult. In the winter, it snows, and it's very windy. Sometimes Julia is scared, but she doesn't come down.

Finally, the lumber company says, "We aren't going to cut down the trees." Then Julia comes down from the tree. Today Julia is still working to save trees. She has a message for every man, woman, and child: Love the trees. Care for our earth.

▶ *What did you read?*

What is this reading about? Circle the best answer.

a. Julia gets up early.

b. Julia wants to save the trees.

c. Julia talks on her cell phone.

▶ *Read again*

Complete these sentences. Circle *a* or *b*.

1. Julia "Butterfly" Hill is	**a.** a young woman.	**b.** an old woman.
2. The lumber company wants	**a.** to cut down trees.	**b.** to save trees.
3. For exercise, Julia	**a.** goes running.	**b.** climbs around in the tree.
4. Many people want to	**a.** learn about her ideas.	**b.** visit her.
5. Julia's friends bring	**a.** breakfast.	**b.** fresh water.

▶ *Show you understand*

Put these sentences in order. Number them from 1–6.

____ She reads letters.

_1_ Julia gets up early.

____ She goes to sleep.

____ She talks on her cell phone.

____ She cooks breakfast.

____ She gets dressed.

▶ *Talk more about it*

Think about these questions. Then talk about your ideas with a partner.

1. How is your day different from Julia's day?
2. Are trees important? Why or why not?

After You Read

▶ *Word search puzzle*

Find these words in the puzzle.

comb	dressed	hair
letters	get	save	write
food	trees	bring

JULIA'S DAY

G	F	E	T	S	A	V	E
L	D	O	W	R	G	E	T
E	C	R	O	R	E	W	R
T	O	J	E	D	I	E	W
T	M	Z	D	S	E	T	S
E	B	Y	O	T	S	R	E
R	H	A	I	R	O	E	Q
S	B	R	I	N	G	W	D

▶ *Write*

Match the words in column A with the words in column B. Write the phrases on the lines. Then use the phrases to complete the letter.

A	B	
1. comb	trees	*comb hair*
2. get	food	_____
3. write	letters	_____
4. bring	hair	_____
5. save	dressed	_____

Dear Lucy,
   I am reading about Julia "Butterfly" Hill. She lives in a tree! In the morning, she _____ fast. Then she *combs* her *hair* .
In the afternoon, she _____. In the evening, her friends _____ and fresh water. Julia is a special young woman. She is working to _____ the _____.
Write back soon!
Your friend,
_____ (sign your name)

READ MORE ABOUT IT

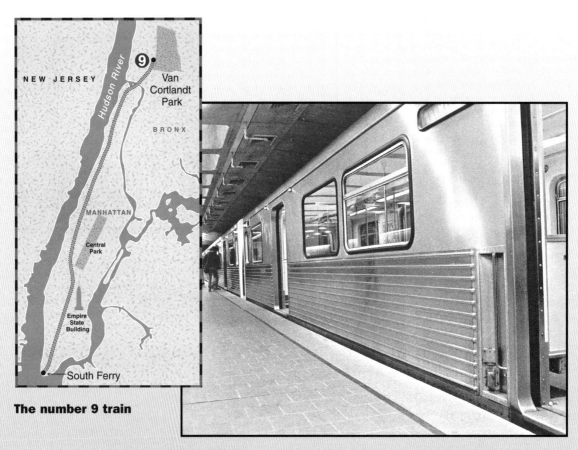

The number 9 train

The subway

Before You Read

Look at the pictures. Look at the title of the reading. Guess the answers to the questions. Circle *a* or *b*.

1. Where does Nick work?

    a. on a subway train   **b**. on a city bus

2. What city does he work in?

    a. New York   **b.** Washington, D.C.

Read this newspaper article. Think about your guesses while you read.

Life Below Ground

Nick works underground all day. He is a conductor on the number 9 subway train in New York City. This train goes from Van Cortlandt Park to South Ferry. Nick opens and closes the train doors. He watches for problems and helps passengers.

This is Nick's day. He wakes up at 4:30 a.m. He takes a shower and gets dressed. There's no time to eat breakfast. At 5:30, he leaves the house and drives to the train station.

At 7:50, he starts his first trip. At each stop he says, "This is the number 9 train to South Ferry. Stand clear of the closing doors, please." He says that 37 times on each trip! At 8:26, he stops at 96th Street.

Many passengers get on here. Teenagers are going to school, and adults are going to work.

There's a middle-aged man with a cup of coffee in his hand. Nick tries to close the doors. The man tries to stop the doors with his coffee cup! The coffee goes everywhere. What a mess!

At 8:58, the train gets to South Ferry. Then Nick takes the train back to Van Cortlandt Park.

He makes this round trip five times every day. His last trip finishes at 1:45 p.m. Then he goes home and cooks dinner. He goes to bed at 9 p.m. He has to get up early!

▶ *What did you read?*

Choose another title for the reading. Circle *a* or *b*.

a. Traveling on the Subway   **b.** Working on the Subway

▶ *Read again*

Are these sentences true? Circle *yes* or *no*.

1. Nick works on the number 2 train.	yes	(no)
2. Nick eats breakfast.	yes	no
3. Many passengers get on at 96th Street.	yes	no
4. Nick makes 10 round trips a day.	yes	no
5. Nick cooks dinner at home.	yes	no

▶ *Scan for numbers*

Scan the reading for times. Complete the sentences with the correct times.

> scan = look quickly to find specific information

1. Nick wakes up at _____.

2. At _____, he leaves the house.

3. He makes his first trip at _____.

4. At about _____, he stops at 96th Street.

5. He finishes his last trip at _____.

▶ *Talk more about it*

Think about these questions. Then talk about your ideas with a partner.

1. How is your day different from Nick's?

2. What do you like about your day?

3. What do you want to change about your day?

 Turn to *Remember the Words*, page 104.

TALK ABOUT IT

A. Work with a small group. Look at the picture in the e-mail. Talk about the family.

Examples: *I think this woman is the grandmother.*
I think the children are cousins.

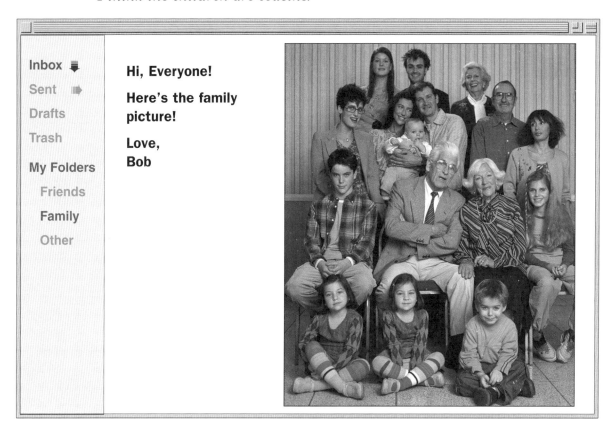

Inbox
Sent
Drafts
Trash

My Folders
  Friends
  Family
  Other

Hi, Everyone!

Here's the family picture!

Love,
Bob

B. Think about these questions. Then talk about your ideas with a partner.

1. Do you have a big family or a small family? Describe some of the people in your family.

2. How do you communicate with your family? Circle your answers.

telephone   letters
e-mail   personal visits

READ ABOUT IT

Before You Read

Look at the pictures. Look at the title of the reading. Guess the answers to the questions. Circle *a* or *b*.

1. Where are the pictures?

   a. on a computer   **b.** in a book

2. What do the photos show?

   a. things people do every day   **b.** important events in people's lives

While You Read

Read this Web page. Think about your guesses while you read.

Teresa's Web Page

Hi! I'm Teresa Salvo-Duarte. Welcome to my Web page. My family is from Brazil, but we live in San Diego now. Look at these pictures. They tell my story.

July 12, 2002 We are moving to California today. My father got a job in San Diego. I'm excited, but I'm also a little worried. I don't have any friends in San Diego.

May 8, 2003 My mother had a baby today. Well, two babies! Twins! I have a new brother and a new sister. My mother is tired, but she's very happy.

September 3, 2002 I'm starting school here today. I'm nervous! I don't know much about the school or the teachers. I'm homesick, too. I miss my friends.

June 11, 2005 Look at me! I am really happy in San Diego now. I graduated from high school today. I'm having a graduation party. All of my friends are here. We are having a great time. But my brother is scared of the music. It is too loud!

▶ What did you read?

What is the reading about? Circle *a* or *b*.

Teresa moved from Brazil to San Diego.

a. She was homesick at first, but now she has friends.

b. She was happy in Brazil, but now she is lonely.

▶ Read again

Are these sentences true? Circle *yes* or *no*.

1. Teresa is in high school now.	yes	(no)
2. The Salvo-Duarte family is from Brazil.	yes	no
3. Teresa's father is working in San Diego.	yes	no
4. Teresa has two sisters.	yes	no
5. Teresa's brother is happy at the graduation party.	yes	no

▶ Show you understand

Put these sentences in order. Number them from 1–5.

___ The twins are born.

___ Teresa graduates from high school.

___ The Salvo-Duarte family moves to the United States.

___ Teresa starts school in San Diego.

_1_ Teresa's father gets a job in San Diego.

▶ Talk more about it

Think about these questions. Talk about your ideas with a partner.

1. Do you like moving to a new place? Why or why not?

2. Is it easy to make new friends? Why or why not?

After You Read

▶ *Words, words, words*

Match the words with the sentences. Write the correct letter in the blank.

_b_ **1.** excited

2. happy

3. homesick

4. tired

5. nervous

a. "I miss my friends and my hometown in Brazil."

b. "I'm graduating today!"

c. "My graduation party went from 8:00 p.m. to midnight. I didn't sleep much."

d. "It's the first day of school, and I don't know any students or teachers here."

e. "My mother had twins, and everyone is fine."

▶ *Write*

List three years. Write a sentence about an event in your life for each year.

Year: *2002*

My sister got married.

Year: _____

_____

Year: _____

_____

Year: _____

_____

READ MORE ABOUT IT

Before You Read

Look at the pictures. Look at the title of the reading. Guess the answers to these questions.

1. What kind of reading is this?

   a. an advertisement   **b.** an interview

2. What is the reading about?

   a. communicating with computers   **b.** buying computers

While You Read

Read the newspaper article. Think about your guesses while you read.

David King... Reporter about Town!

Today's topic: **Computer Talk**

David King: Do you use the computer to communicate with family and friends?

 Sara Yee: No, I don't. I don't have a computer. I'm a little scared of them. Also, I work a lot. I don't have time to learn about computers. I call people on the telephone, or I write letters—with a pen!

 Oleg Lednev: Yes, I do. I send birthday cards to all my friends. It's quick and easy. I send graduation cards and funny cards, too. I save a lot of money on cards!

 Carlos Quinto: Yes, I do. My family is in Mexico. Sometimes I'm very homesick. Now I have a computer, and I can e-mail them every day. Telephone calls were very expensive, but e-mail is cheap for me!

 Regina Ramos: Oh, yes! I talk to my grandchildren in Caracas online. We send instant messages. I write slowly on the computer, but I try! I also order presents online for my grandchildren.

Next week, David King interviews people about their jobs. Maybe he'll talk to YOU!

▶ *Read again*

How do the people in the reading communicate with family and friends? Mark (✗) the way they DON'T mention.

___ **1.** send e-mail messages

___ **2.** write letters (with pen and paper)

___ **3.** order presents online

___ **4.** send birthday cards online

___ **5.** mail packages at the post office

___ **6.** make telephone calls

___ **7.** "talk" with instant messages

▶ *Show you understand*

Read these sentences. Then write *Sara, Carlos, Oleg,* or *Regina* in the blank.

1. This person has grandchildren in Caracas. _____

2. This person doesn't have a computer. _____

3. This person's family is in Mexico. _____

4. This person saves money on birthday cards. _____

▶ *Talk more about it*

Think about these questions. Then ask and answer the questions with a partner.

> **1.** How many letters do you write (with a pen or pencil) in one year?
>
> **2.** Do you use e-mail? Why or why not?
>
> **3.** When do you send people special cards?

 Turn to *Remember the Words,* page 104.

TALK ABOUT IT

A. What parts of the house do you see in the picture? Mark (✗) them.

___ carpet	___ closet	___ deck
___ door	___ floor	___ roof
___ shower	___ window	___ wall

B. Think about these questions. Then talk about your ideas with a partner.

> **1.** A tree house is an unusual house. Can you name other unusual houses?
>
> **2.** Do you like big houses? Do you like small houses? Why?

READ ABOUT IT

Before You Read

Look at the pictures. Look at the title of the reading. Guess the answers to the questions. Circle *yes* or *no*.

1. Can people move yurts easily?   yes   no

2. Is it difficult to build a yurt?   yes   no

While You Read

Read the magazine article. Think about your guesses while you read.

A Yurt: A Home to Go

What is a yurt?

A yurt is a large round tent. Yurts are from Mongolia originally, but today there are yurts all over the world. A yurt is portable. People can move it from one place to another place.

Building a yurt

Janet Daley and her friends are building her yurt. They don't need many tools to build a yurt. They need just a few things like a tape measure, a saw, a hammer and nails, and a screwdriver and screws.

First, Janet and her friends make the round floor. They measure the floor carefully. It has to be exactly the right size. Second, the walls and the door go up. Some yurts have windows. They put the windows in at this time, too.

Next, Janet and her friends put on the roof. Then they make a wooden deck for the front of the yurt.

Finally, they cover the yurt with a heavy cloth. Now Janet's yurt is ready. She can move in. ■

▶ *What did you read?*

What is this reading about? Circle the best answer.

a. building a yurt   **b.** living in a yurt

▶ *Read again*

Read these sentences. Which sentences are correct? Circle *a* or *b*.

1. a. Yurts are round.   **b.** Yurts are square.

2. a. It's easy to move a yurt.   **b.** It's difficult to move a yurt.

3. a. Only people in Mongolia live in yurts.   **b.** People in many countries live in yurts.

4. a. Builders make the deck of the yurt first.   **b.** Builders make the floor of the yurt first.

5. a. All yurts have windows.   **b.** Some yurts have windows.

▶ *Show you understand*

Put these sentences in order. Number them from 1–5.

____ Move into the yurt.

____ Make the floor of the yurt.

____ Put the roof on.

____ Put the deck on the front of the yurt.

____ Put up the walls and door.

▶ *Talk more about it*

Think about these questions. Then ask and answer the questions with a partner.

1. Are yurts good houses for everyone? Why or why not?

2. Is a yurt a good house for you? Why or why not?

After You Read

▶ *Words, words, words*

Read these sentences. Fill in the blanks with words from the box.

tent	cloth	floor	hammer	tape measure

1. Please, measure the door carefully. Use this _____.
2. Please, put those boxes on the _____ over there.
3. We can spend a night in the mountains. I have a new _____.
4. Let's put up this picture. Give me the _____ and some nails, please.
5. They're covering the yurt with a heavy _____.

▶ *Write*

Write about your home. Answer these questions. Then write your answers in paragraph form. Use the lines below.

Where do you live?

What does your home look like?

Who do you live with?

I live _____

_____

_____

_____

_____

_____

_____

I live at 23 Jancey Avenue. I live in the red brick building. I live with my sister, her husband, and their children.

READ MORE ABOUT IT

Before You Read

Look at the picture and the title of the reading. Guess the answer to the question. Circle *a* or *b*.

What do the people want to do?

a. They want to ride on a boat.

b. They want to live on a boat.

While You Read

Read the advertisement. Think about your guess while you read.

At Home on a Houseboat!

Come join the community at Cabin Crest. Enjoy the beautiful view from your own houseboat. There are new houseboats for sale at this time.

Features of our houseboats

- Two bedrooms with large closets
- One bathroom with sink, toilet, and shower
- Living room with two bookcases
- Carpet in all living areas (except the kitchen)
- Kitchen with new appliances (stove, oven, microwave, refrigerator/freezer)

Features of our friendly community

- Driveway and parking area near the houseboats
- Garbage collection
- Children's play area
- Community center with activities for everyone!
- Call today for a tour of one of our houseboats: 555-2743

▶ *What did you read?*

The words in the box make a sentence about the reading. Put them in order. Write the sentence on the line.

houseboat	life	a
is	on	good

_____

▶ *Read again*

Do the houseboats at Cabin Crest have these things? Mark (✗) the boxes in the chart.

Feature	YES	NO
1. two bedrooms		
2. two bathrooms		
3. carpet in kitchen		
4. garbage collection		
5. free cleaning service		

▶ *Show you understand*

Read the questions. Complete the answers with words from the reading.

1. Where are the closets?   They're in the _____.

2. Where is the shower?   It's in the _____.

3. Where is the stove?   It's in the _____.

4. Where are the bookcases?   They're in the _____.

5. Where is the parking area?   It's near the _____.

▶ *Talk more about it*

Think about these questions. Then talk about your ideas with a partner.

> **1.** Who wants to live on a houseboat? Circle your answers.
>
>   single people   large families   older people   students
>
> **2.** Where do you want to live? Why?

 Turn to *Remember the Words*, page 104.

Shop Smart!

TALK ABOUT IT

A. Look at the picture. Complete the chart with the items in the box.

cheese	lamb	butter	peaches	spinach	turkey

What do you usually buy in these aisles? Write two more items on each list below.

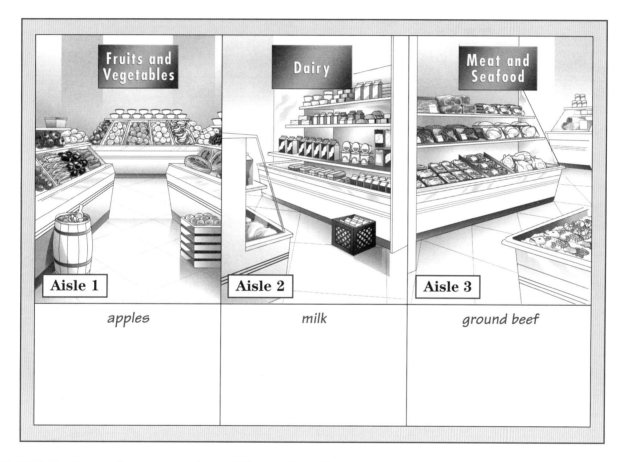

Aisle 1	Aisle 2	Aisle 3
apples	milk	ground beef

B. Think about these questions. Then ask and answer the questions with a partner.

1. What are some foods that you never buy? Why don't you buy them?

2. Do you buy food at other kinds of food stores? Fruit and vegetable markets? Fish markets?

Before You Read

Look at these pictures. Guess the answer to the question. Circle *a* or *b*.

Which picture matches the title "Smart Supermarket Shopping"?

a.

b.

While You Read

Read this magazine article. Think about your guess while you read.

Smart Supermarket Shopping

Smart shoppers save time and money. Are you a smart shopper?

When do you shop?

The best time to shop is in the morning. The shelves are full. The aisles aren't crowded.

The fruits and vegetables are fresh. The checkout is fast.

Where do you shop?

Pick the best supermarket for you. Many people like a supermarket near their home.

Walk around with your shopping cart. Can you find your favorite cereal or soup?

Is there a salad bar? Is the fish fresh?

Go to the cash register. Does the checker greet each customer? Does the packer carry their bags?

How do you shop?

Make a shopping list. Don't buy extra groceries. Choose healthy foods. Don't shop when you are hungry. Eat an apple or a sandwich before you shop.

How do you save money?

Be a smart shopper. Save money with coupons. Recycle cans and bottles. Choose store brands for bread, pasta, and yogurt. Look for special sales. "Buy one carton of milk, and the second one is free!"

Do you need to go shopping today? Make a list. Go to the supermarket. Get a shopping cart and SHOP!

▶ What did you read?

What is this reading about? Circle *a* or *b*.

The article tells people how to…

a. save money at the supermarket.   **b.** get a job at the supermarket.

▶ Read again

Are these good ideas for smart shoppers? Circle *yes* or *no*.

1. Shop in the morning.	(yes)	no
2. Choose a good supermarket for you.	yes	no
3. Shop when you are hungry.	yes	no
4. Buy a lot of extra groceries.	yes	no
5. Use coupons.	yes	no

▶ Show you understand

Find words in the reading for these categories. Write them in the chart.

FOOD	PEOPLE	MONEY SAVERS
fruits	*checker*	*coupons*

▶ Talk more about it

Think about these questions. Then ask and answer the questions with a partner.

1. Do you shop at a supermarket near your house?

2. When do you shop?

3. How do you save money at the supermarket?

After You Read

▶ *Write*

You are cooking dinner for a friend. Write a menu and a shopping list. Try to use two (or more) of the Rainbow Market specials!

Dinner Menu

Shopping List

Rainbow Market
SPECIAL SALES THIS WEEK

- -

Rainbow Market Bread $1.29

- -

Ground beef . . . .$1.59 per pound

- -

Rainbow Market
    Onion Soup . . . .$1.29 a can

- -

Apples . . . .$2.99 for a bag

- -

Lucky Farms Milk . .$1.79 one half gallon*
    *Buy one, get one free

- -

Imported Italian cheese . .$5.49 per pound

- -

Rainbow Market Pasta . . . .$ .99

- -

▶ *Supermarket Tic Tac Toe*

Play with a partner. Choose a word. Then say a sentence with the word. Is your sentence correct? You get the square.

coupons	shop	aisle
shelves	bag	carton
sale	customer	recycle

READ MORE ABOUT IT

Before You Read

Look at the pictures. Look at the title of the reading. Guess the answers to the questions. Circle *a* or *b*.

1. What is this reading about?   **a.** food labels   **b.** food coupons
2. How do you choose healthy foods?   **a.** compare prices   **b.** compare ingredients

While You Read

Read the brochure. Think about your guesses while you read.

Read for Your Health!

Food labels give you important information. They list the ingredients in foods, and they tell you nutrition facts about the foods. Some foods are not very healthy. They contain a lot of fat, sugar, and salt (sodium). It isn't a good idea to eat a lot of these things. Other foods are low in fat, sugar, and salt. Compare these two brands of pizza. You can see the difference.

PAPA'S REAL PIZZA

SAUSAGE PIZZA

Papa makes it … the way you love it!
Lots of cheese! Lots of sausage!

Nutrition Facts
Serving Size: 1 slice

Calories: 448

Total Fat: 21 g.

Sodium: 1,115 mg.

Sugar: 6 g.

Ingredients: flour, water, tomatoes, cheese, sausage, oil, salt, garlic

Maria's Healthy Pizza

Spinach-Mushroom Pizza

Good . . . and healthy!
Low in fat!
Low in sugar and salt!

Ingredients: flour, water, tomatoes, spinach, mushrooms, onions, cheese, oil, garlic, salt

Nutrition Facts
Serving Size: 1 slice

Calories: 330

Total Fat: 13 g.

Sodium: 500 mg.

Sugar: 4 g.

▶ Read again

Read the sentences. Which pizza does each person want? Mark (X) the correct box in the chart.

	PAPA'S	MARIA'S
Brad: Let's get pizza for dinner. I want a pizza with meat.		
Erin: Pizza sounds good. But I don't eat meat.		
Marisa: I want pizza. But I'm on a diet.		
Paul: I'm not on a diet. And I really don't like spinach!		

▶ Scan for numbers

Read these sentences. Then scan the pizza labels. Look for the numbers to complete the sentences.

> scan = look quickly to find specific information

1. A slice of Papa's pizza has _____ calories; a slice of Maria's pizza has _____ calories.

2. A slice of Papa's pizza has _____ grams of fat; a slice of Maria's pizza has _____ grams of fat.

3. One slice of Papa's pizza has _____ mg. of sodium; a slice of Maria's Pizza has _____ mg. of sodium.

▶ Talk more about it

Think about these questions. Then ask and answer the questions with a partner.

1. How do you shop? Do you compare prices? Do you compare ingredients?

2. What foods have a lot of fat, sugar, or salt? Do you eat some of these foods?

3. What healthy foods do you eat?

 Turn to *Remember the Words*, page 104.

Let's Eat Out

TALK ABOUT IT

A. Work with a partner. Guess the answers to the questions. Circle *a*, *b*, or *c*.

Test Your "Eating-Out IQ"

1. Which meal do people eat
out most often?
a. breakfast
b. lunch
c. dinner

2. Where do people eat out
most often?
a. fast-food restaurants
b. sit-down restaurants
c. grocery stores

3. What is the most popular
menu item?
a. hot dog
b. pizza
c. french fries

4. What is the most popular day
to eat out for breakfast?
a. Friday
b. Saturday
c. Sunday

5. Who eats out most often?
a. teenagers
b. adult men
c. adult women

(Check the answers on page 40.)

B. Think about these questions. Then ask and answer the questions with a partner.

1. Which meal do you eat out most often? Why?

2. Where do you eat out most often? At fast-food restaurants?
At sit-down restaurants?

3. What do you usually order in restaurants?

READ ABOUT IT

Before You Read

Look at the pictures. Look at the title of the reading. Guess the answers to the questions. Circle *a* or *b*.

1. What does Norma do?

    a. She works in a restaurant.   **b.** She writes for a newspaper.

2. What kind of a restaurant is Nat's?

    a. It's a fast-food restaurant.   **b.** It's a coffee shop.

While You Read

Read this newspaper article. Think about your guesses while you read.

Norma's Restaurant Review

DO YOU LIKE TO EAT OUT? Try a meal at Nat's Early Bite Coffee Shop. Nat's is not a fancy restaurant. The place mats are paper, and the napkins are, too. But the food is good, the service is fast, and everybody is friendly.

Let me describe a visit to Nat's. A friendly waitress takes me to a table. A busboy comes and puts a place mat and silverware on the table. The waitress brings me a menu. A minute later, she brings me a glass of water. The service here is very good.

I look around. The restaurant is busy. There are people at every table and in every booth. People say the best meal here is breakfast. I look at all the menu items. Scrambled eggs and toast. Pancakes and syrup. Hmm! It's hard to decide.

Then I see a large sign on the cashier's counter. It says, "Today's Special—Breakfast Burrito." My waitress comes back. She asks, "Are you ready to order?" I ask, "What's in the Breakfast Burrito?" She says, "It has sausage, onions, peppers, potatoes, and cheese. My customers love it."

I order the breakfast burrito, orange juice, and a cup of coffee. My breakfast arrives in five minutes. It looks great. I pick up my fork. I take a bite. It's delicious!

▶ *What did you read?*

What is this reading about? Circle the best answer.

a. Nat's is a friendly restaurant with good food.

b. Nat's is very busy at breakfast time.

▶ *Read again*

Read these sentences. Which sentences are correct? Circle *a* or *b*.

1. **a.** Nat's is a fancy restaurant.
   b. Nat's isn't a fancy restaurant.

2. **a.** A busboy brings a place mat.
   b. A busboy brings a menu.

3. **a.** People say the best meal is breakfast.
   b. People say the best meal is lunch.

4. **a.** Norma orders pancakes and syrup.
   b. Norma orders a burrito.

5. **a.** The restaurant is busy.
   b. There aren't many people in the restaurant.

6. **a.** The waitress brings Norma some tea.
   b. The waitress brings Norma a glass of water.

▶ *Show you understand*

Find words in the reading for these categories. Write them in the chart.

PEOPLE	FOOD	THINGS ON THE TABLE
waitress	scrambled eggs	place mats

▶ *Talk more about it*

Think about these questions. Then ask and answer the questions with a partner.

1. What is your favorite restaurant? Why?
2. What is more important—good food or good service? Why?
3. Do you know anyone who works in a restaurant? What job do they do?

After You Read

▶ *Words, words, words*

Read these sentences. What do the underlined words mean? Circle *a* or *b*.

1. The busboy brings <u>silverware</u>.

    a. fork and spoon   **b.** plate and cup

2. Are you ready to <u>order</u>?

    a. say what you want to eat   **b.** say where you want to sit

3. <u>Nat's Early Bite Coffee Shop</u> is a <u>popular</u> restaurant.

    a. Many people work there.   **b.** Many people eat there.

4. Can I please see a <u>menu</u>?

    a. a list of food and prices   **b.** a check you have to pay

5. My <u>customers</u> love it.

    a. people who work in the restaurant   **b.** people who eat in the restaurant

▶ *Word forms: plurals with -s and -es*

Complete the chart with singular or plural forms.

SINGULAR	PLURAL
waitress	
	glasses
potato	
	busboys
cup	
	onions

Choose two plural words from the chart. Write a sentence with each one.

1. _____

2. _____

READ MORE ABOUT IT

Before You Read

Look at the pictures. Look at the title of the reading. Guess the answers to the questions. Circle *a* or *b*.

1. What meal is this menu for?

   a. breakfast   **b.** lunch

2. What does the menu include?

   a. eggs   **b.** sandwiches

While You Read

Read the menu. Think about your guesses while you read.

BREAKFAST AT NAT'S

We serve breakfast all day! We bake everything here!

Today's Special: Breakfast Burrito $5.25

MENU

Main courses

3 pancakes with syrup...$4.50

2 eggs (scrambled or fried) and toast.................$3.50

Omelet (3 eggs) and toast...................................$4.00
   Choice of filling: cheese, ham, onion,   (add $.50 for
   green pepper, tomato   each filling)

The Every Day Special.....................................$6.00
2 eggs (scrambled or fried), toast,
bacon or sausage, coffee, juice

Side orders

Bacon or sausage...$2.00

Muffin..$1.25

Beverages

Coffee or tea..$1.25

Milk, small or large...$.75/$1.50

Juice (orange, grapefruit, apple), small or large.. $1.25/$2.00

You can order from our lunch menu after 11:30 a.m.

▶ Read again

Are these sentences true? Circle *yes* or *no*.

1. You can eat breakfast foods at 3 p.m.   yes   no
2. Nat's Early Bite Coffee Shop bakes its own bread.   yes   no
3. You can get the Burrito Special every day.   yes   no
4. The Every Day Special has bacon or sausage.   yes   no
5. Nat's Early Bite Coffee Shop serves lunch.   yes   no

▶ Show you understand

Look at the menu. Write the prices in Guest Checks 1 and 2. How much does each order cost?

Guest Check #1	
1	breakfast burrito special $5.25
1	every day special (with fried eggs, bacon, coffee, orange juice) _____
1	small orange juice _____
1	coffee _____
	Total: _____

Guest Check #2	
1	pancakes with syrup _____
1	side order of bacon _____
1	large milk _____
1	omelet with cheese and ham _____
2	cups of coffee _____
	Total: _____

Guest Check #3	
	Total: _____

▶ Write

You have $12.00. Order your breakfast from Nat's menu. Write your order in Guest Check 3. Make sure it costs $12.00 or less.

 Turn to *Remember the Words*, page 104.

(Answers to quiz on page 35: **1.** *b* **2.** *a* **3.** *c* **4.** *c* **5.** *a)*

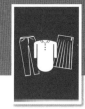

Working Clothes

TALK ABOUT IT

A. Look at the outfits in the pictures. Write the names of the clothes you know.

Business clothes

suit

_____

_____

A casual outfit

_____

_____

_____

Designer clothes

_____

_____

_____

B. Think about these questions. Talk about your ideas with a partner.

1. Which kind of clothes do you wear most? When do you wear them?

   business   casual   designer

2. Which kind of clothes do you <u>like</u> most? When do you wear them?

   business   casual   designer

READ ABOUT IT

Before You Read

Look at the picture. Look at the title of the reading. Guess which words are in the reading. Mark (✗) them.

___ sew   ___ design   ___ living room

___ sofa   ___ outfit   ___ shoes

While You Read

Read the magazine article. Check your guesses.

Art Student to Fashion Designer

Cynthia Rowley is a fashion designer. This is her story.

It's the 1980s. Cynthia Rowley is a student at the Art Institute of Chicago. One day her roommate has an idea. She says, "You like to draw, and you like to sew. Be a fashion designer!" Cynthia likes the idea.

Cynthia gets a sewing machine, some needles, some thread, and some material. She designs outfits for women. Then she makes and wears her outfits.

One day, Cynthia is riding on the train. A manager from a famous department store sees her. She likes Cynthia's clothes. The manager stops Cynthia and asks, "Who makes your clothes?" Cynthia says, "I do. I'm a fashion designer." Then the manager says, "Please bring some of your clothes to the store on Monday morning."

Cynthia works all weekend. She makes five new outfits. The people at the department store love her clothes. Cynthia's career as a fashion designer begins!

Now Cynthia Rowley is a famous fashion designer. She has stores in New York, Los Angeles, Chicago, and Japan. She designs clothes for men and women. She also designs shoes, purses, wallets, watches, eyeglasses, gloves, and umbrellas. You can find her clothing in many places!

▶ What did you read?

The words in the box make a sentence about the reading. Put them in order. Write the sentence on the line.

| fashion designer | A | begins | career | her |

_____

▶ Read again

Complete the answers to these questions.

1. Cynthia Rowley is a student. What does she like to do?

She likes to _____ and _____.

2. Who does Cynthia meet on the train?

She meets the _____ of a famous _____ _____.

3. How many outfits does Cynthia make over the weekend?

She makes _____ _____.

4. Cynthia Rowley designs clothes. What are three other things she designs?

She also designs _____, _____, and _____.

▶ Show you understand

Put the sentences in order. Number them from 1–5.

____ She listens to her roommate's idea and starts to design clothes.

____ Cynthia becomes a famous fashion designer.

_1_ Cynthia Rowley goes to art school.

____ She brings her clothes to the department store.

____ She meets a department store manager on the train.

▶ Talk more about it

Think about these questions. Then ask and answer the questions with a partner.

1. Are you interested in fashion design? Why or why not?

2. Name some famous fashion designers. What do they design?

After You Read

▶ *Words, words, words*

Read the sentences. What do the underlined words mean? Circle *a* or *b*.

1. Cynthia Rowley <u>designs</u> clothes.

    a. plans and makes   **b.** buys and sells

2. She can <u>sew</u> very well. She makes beautiful clothes.

    a. measure with a ruler   **b.** put together with thread

3. Cynthia works every day. She likes her <u>career</u>.

    a. job   **b.** company

4. Fashion designers <u>draw</u> their clothes first. Then they sew them.

    a. take pictures with a camera   **b.** make pictures with a pen or pencil

▶ *Write*

Design a piece of clothing. Draw a picture of it. Answer the questions. Write your answers in paragraph form. Use the lines below.

What is it?

Is it for a man, a woman, or both?

Is it designer, business, or casual clothing?

What color is it?

_____

_____

_____

_____

_____

_____

_____

This is a jacket. It's for a man or for a woman. It's casual clothing. It's red and gray.

Before You Read

Look at the pictures. Look at the title of the article. Guess the answer to the question.

How much did this woman's clothing cost?

a. $0.00   **b.** $50.00   **c.** $150.00

While You Read

Read the newspaper article. Think about your guess while you read.

Free Work Clothes

Imagine this: You don't have a job. Or maybe you have a job, but you don't make much money. You can get a good job, but you have one problem. You don't have nice clothes for work. You don't have nice clothes for an interview. What can you do?

In Cincinnati, Ohio, this isn't a problem. You can go to Back on Track Workwear. At Back on Track Workwear, the clothes are free for working people. They are also free for people with job interviews. Back on Track Workwear has suits, ties, dresses, skirts, pants, shirts, and blouses. It also has white uniforms for medical workers. It has clothes in all sizes, from small to extra-large.

The shoppers at Back on Track Workwear can take several blouses or shirts, skirts or pants, shoes, suits, and ties. Then they are ready for work, or an important interview.

Back on Track Workwear helps people get a job and keep a job.

▶ *What did you read?*

What is the reading about? Circle *a*, *b*, or *c*.

a. free clothes for working people

b. the right clothes for a job interview

c. stores for businesspeople

▶ *Read again*

Read these sentences. Which sentences are correct? Circle *a* or *b*.

1. a. Shoppers don't pay for clothes. **b.** Shoppers pay a little for clothes.

2. a. People can't get clothes for interviews. **b.** People can get clothes for interviews.

3. a. People can get uniforms. **b.** There are no uniforms.

4. a. People can get bathing suits. **b.** There are only clothes for work.

5. a. Shoppers can get only one outfit. **b.** Shoppers can get more than one outfit.

▶ *Words, words, words*

Look at the reading. Underline words for men's clothes and women's clothes. Then write the words in this chart. Compare your answers with a partner. Do you agree?

Clothes for men	
Clothes for women	
Clothes for both	

▶ *Talk more about it*

Think about these questions. Talk about your ideas with a partner.

1. Is there a place like Back on Track Workwear in your community? Tell about it.

2. What do you wear to a job interview? At home? For school?

 Turn to *Remember the Words*, page 104.

TALK ABOUT IT

A. Label the photos with words from the box. Talk about the pictures with a partner. What do you see in the pictures? What are the people doing?

hospital	doctor's office	pharmacy

_____   _____   _____

B. Think about these questions. Then ask and answer the questions with your partner.

1. Where are the pharmacies in your community?

2. Where do you go in an emergency?

3. Is there a hospital near your house?

READ ABOUT IT

Before You Read

Look at the pictures. Look at the title of the article. Guess the answers to the questions. Circle *a*, *b*, or *c*.

1. The woman is ready for work. What is her job?

    a. receptionist   **b.** nurse   **c.** doctor

2. What does the word *barter* mean?

    a. to buy something   **b.** to buy something   **c.** to get something
        with money   without money   for free

While You Read

Read this newspaper article. Think about your guesses while you read.

The Barter Clinic

Meet Dr. Susan Osborne. Every day at work, she examines patients. She gives shots, and she writes prescriptions. Susan Osborne is a doctor, but she is an unusual doctor. She never wears a white coat. She greets her patients in the waiting room, and she often spends more than an hour with her patients. Also, a visit to Dr. Osborne's office is not expensive.

The name of Dr. Osborne's office is "The Barter Clinic." This means that not all patients pay her with money. Of course, some patients pay with money, but patients can also "barter" for their health care. This means that they pay with other things. Some patients do work for her. They paint or repair things in the office. Other patients pay with fruit, vegetables, chickens, or eggs, for example.

Dr. Osborne doesn't make a lot of money, but she is happy about her career. She makes a difference in people's lives.

Barter Clinic

1 Doctor's visit..........
1 Flu shot...............
Total charges: 3 hours painting

▶ *What did you read?*

Choose another title for the reading. Circle the best one.

a. Expensive Health Care

b. An Unusual Health Care System

c. A Free Health Care System

▶ *Read again*

Are these sentences true? Circle *yes* or *no*.

1. Many doctors are like Susan Osborne.	yes	no
2. Dr. Osborne spends a lot of time with her patients.	yes	no
3. Patients can pay Dr. Osborne with food.	yes	no
4. Dr. Osborne makes a lot of money.	yes	no
5. Dr. Osborne likes her work.	yes	no

▶ *Show you understand*

Read the list of things that Dr. Osborne does. Mark (✗) the unusual things.

___ **1.** She doesn't wear a white coat.

___ **2.** She greets patients in the waiting room.

___ **3.** She writes prescriptions.

___ **4.** She gives shots.

___ **5.** She spends an hour or more with patients.

___ **6.** She takes work or other things for pay.

▶ *Talk more about it*

Think about these questions. Then ask and answer the questions with a partner.

> **1.** Is your doctor like Dr. Osborne? Explain.
>
> **2.** Do you know anyone who barters for anything? Talk about him or her.

After You Read

▶ *Words, words, words*

Read these sentences. What do the underlined words mean? Circle *a* or *b*.

1. Dr. Osborne examines all of her <u>patients</u> very carefully.

    a. medical books   **b.** people who visit a doctor

2. Dr. Osborne <u>greets</u> everyone in the waiting room.

    a. says *hello* to   **b.** examines

3. Dr. Osborne gives <u>shots</u> and writes prescriptions.

    a. time   **b.** injections

4. Patients can <u>repair</u> things to pay for Dr. Osborne's care.

    a. buy   **b.** fix

5. Most people cannot <u>barter</u> for their medical care.

    a. pay with money   **b.** pay without money

▶ *Write*

Read the paragraph. Complete Hannah Park's medical form with information from the box.

Hannah Park lives at 243 Munson Avenue in San Francisco, California. Her phone number is 555-2850. She is 60 years old. She is going to the doctor today. She has high blood pressure. She takes medicine for it every day. Today she is seeing the doctor about a sore throat. She is coughing a lot. She also feels tired.

Westward Medical
Patient Information Form

Name: *Hannah Park*

Sex (circle):   Male   Female

Age: ____

Address: _____

Phone number: _____

Are you taking any medicines now? (circle)

   Yes   Why are you taking this medicine?

     I'm taking it for _____

   No

Why are you seeing the doctor today?

_____

READ MORE ABOUT IT

Before You Read

Look at the picture. Look at the title of the reading. Guess which words are in the reading. Mark (✗) them.

___ exercise   ___ head   ___ sew   ___ tool   ___ high blood pressure

___ medicine   ___ mirror   ___ problem   ___ hair   ___ stomach

While You Read

Read the brochure. Check your guesses while you read.

What Doctors Ask

What to expect at the doctor's office

Are you ready to visit the doctor's office? Are you nervous? Sometimes it is difficult to explain your problem. Don't worry. These questions can help you.

Doctors often ask:

1. What is the problem?

2. Where does it hurt? (your stomach? your shoulder?)

3. Is this a new medical problem?

4. What are you feeling right now? (a headache? a sore throat?)

5. What makes you feel better? (a heating pad? rest?)

6. What makes you feel worse? (exercise? coughing?)

7. What medicines are you taking now?

8. Do you have any other health problems? (high blood pressure?)

9. How often do you exercise?

▶ *What did you read?*

Who is the brochure for? Circle *a* or *b*.

a. doctors   **b.** patients

▶ *Read again*

Match the questions and answers.

___ **1.** Where does it hurt?

___ **2.** What makes you feel better?

___ **3.** Are you taking any medicine now?

___ **4.** Do you have any other health problems?

___ **5.** Do you exercise regularly?

a. Rest helps a lot.

b. My neck and my shoulder hurt.

c. Yes, I run every day.

d. No, my health is good.

e. No, I'm not taking any medicine now.

▶ *Words, words, words*

Read the sentences. Fill in the blanks with the words in the box.

exercise	coughing	shoulder	medicine	headache

1. I can't move my arm. My _____ hurts.

2. I _____ every day. It makes me feel good.

3. Don't turn the radio on. I have a _____.

4. Get him some water, please. He's _____ a lot.

5. My aunt takes _____ every day for her high blood pressure.

▶ *Talk more about it*

Think about these questions. Then talk about your ideas with a partner.

> **1.** Some people are nervous about visiting the doctor. Why?
>
> **2.** Do you think the questions in the brochure are helpful? Why or why not?

 Turn to *Remember the Words*, page 104.

TALK ABOUT IT

A. Work in a small group. Look at the chart and the photos. Mark (✗) to complete the chart. Talk about your answers with your group.

Where do you find...	BIG CITY	SMALL TOWN	BOTH
friendly people?			
helpful neighbors?			
busy and crowded streets?			
parks and gardens?			
interesting places to visit?			
a lot of tall buildings?			

B. Think about these questions. Then ask and answer the questions with your group.

1. Do you like big cities or small towns? Why?
2. What do you like best about your community?

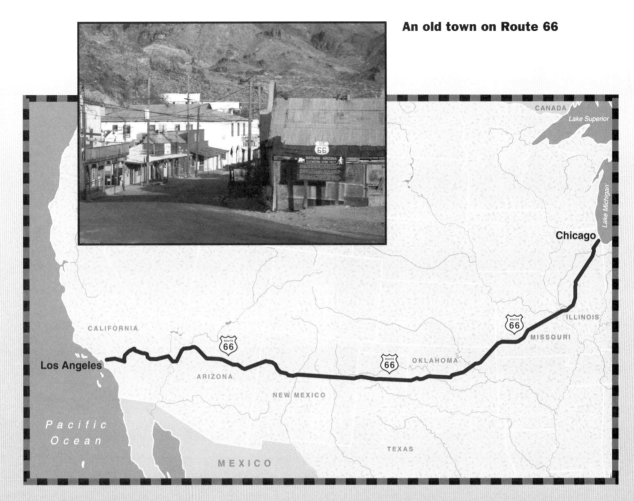

An old town on Route 66

A map of Route 66

Before You Read

Look at the pictures. Look at the title of the reading. Guess the answers to the questions. Circle *a* or *b*.

1. What is Keiko writing?

    a. a journal of a trip   **b.** a letter to a friend

2. Where is she going?

    a. only to Chicago   **b.** to many U.S. towns

While You Read

Read about Keiko's trip. Think about your guesses while you read.

A Trip on Route 66

April 2nd
My friends and I are at a bus station in Chicago, Illinois. We are waiting for the bus. We're all very excited about our Route 66 trip. Route 66 opened in 1926. It starts here and goes to Los Angeles, California. It is about 2,400 miles long. It crosses 8 states. In 1970, a bigger highway opened. Then people stopped using Route 66. Many towns died, but there are still many interesting small towns on this road.

April 12th
We're in Adrian, Texas, at the Midpoint Café. This is exactly halfway between Chicago and Los Angeles. These days, Adrian is a small and quiet town. About 150 people live here. There aren't many stores, but there's a bakery with great apple pie!

April 20th
I'm in "Standin' on the Corner Park" in Winslow, Arizona. Yes, that IS the name of the park. The name comes from a famous song called "Take It Easy." At the corner, there's a bench and a statue on the sidewalk. Winslow is a popular town with tourists on Route 66.

Well, my trip ends in a few days in Los Angeles. I have a package to mail there—some Route 66 T-shirts for my family and friends!

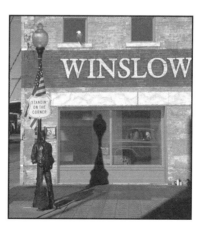

▶ What did you read?

The words in the box make a sentence about the reading. Put them in order. Write the sentence on the line.

| interesting | an | Keiko | trip | on Route 66 | is taking |

_____

▶ Read again

Are these sentences true? Circle *yes* or *no*.

1. Route 66 is a new highway.	yes	(no)
2. Today most people use a different highway.	yes	no
3. Adrian, Texas, is about 2,400 miles from Chicago.	yes	no
4. Winslow, Arizona, is a popular town for tourists.	yes	no
5. Some towns on Route 66 died.	yes	no

▶ Show you understand

Which states are these places in? Mark (✗) the correct boxes.

Places on Route 66	ILLINOIS	TEXAS	ARIZONA	CALIFORNIA
Chicago	✗			
Standin' on the Corner Park				
The Midpoint Café				
Los Angeles				
Winslow				

▶ Talk more about it

Think about these questions. Then ask and answer the questions with a partner.

1. Do you want to travel on Route 66? Why or why not?
2. What states in the United States do you want to see? Why?
3. Which do you prefer—to travel by car or to travel by bus? Why?

After You Read

▶ *Scan for numbers*

Scan the reading for the numbers in the box. Then complete each sentence with the correct number.

> scan = look quickly to find specific information

| 1970 | 8 | 2,400 | 150 | 1926 | 12 |

1. Route 66 is _____ miles long.

2. Route 66 crosses _____ states.

3. Route 66 opened in _____.

4. A bigger highway opened in _____.

5. Adrian, Texas, has about _____ people.

6. Keiko was in Adrian on April _____.

▶ *Write*

A. Read Keiko's postcard.

April 24

Dear Ben,
Greetings from Los Angeles! The weather here is sunny and warm. Today I'm visiting a movie studio in Hollywood. Tomorrow I want to go to the beach.
 See you soon!
 Keiko

Ben Chan
 5 Sev
Chicago, 1

B. Imagine you are on a trip. Complete the postcard.

_____

Dear _____,
Greetings from _____!
The weather here is

_____.
Today I'm _____.
Tomorrow I want to
_____. See you soon!

_____

A community garden

A block party

Before You Read

Work with a small group. Look at the pictures. Guess the answers to these questions.

1. What are the people doing?

2. Are they family or neighbors?

Read this newspaper article. Think about your guesses while you read.

Neighbor to Neighbor

What is a community? Twelve-year-old Sophie knows. She says, "It's not only your school or the mall. A community is a lot of people helping each other."

Neighbors help each other in many ways. In Seattle, George builds new benches for the neighborhood, and Cindy plants trees along the sidewalks. Now people come out of their homes. They sit and talk. They spend time together.

In Detroit, Lillian and her neighbors turn empty parking lots into community gardens. They grow fruit and vegetables.

People want safe communities. In Atlanta, Rosa and her neighbors meet every month.

They have a neighborhood watch group. They ask police and fire fighters to speak to their group. Together, they stop robberies and prevent fires.

People also want clean communities. In New York, neighbors clean up parks and train stations. School and church groups also clean up neighborhood streets.

Good neighbors have fun together. Sophie's family puts a basketball net on their corner.

Now there are games after dinner. There is a block party every summer. Each family brings food. There is music and dancing.

What makes a great community? Neighbors helping neighbors. Neighbors like you!

▶ *What did you read?*

What is this reading about? Circle *a* or *b*.

a. great parties   **b.** great neighborhoods

▶ *Read again*

Complete these sentences. Circle *a* or *b*.

1. In a great community,   **a.** there are big malls.   **b.** neighbors help each other.

2. Good neighbors   **a.** don't talk to each other.   **b.** spend some time together.

3. Neighborhood watch groups   **a.** meet to talk about safety.   **b.** meet to keep parks clean.

4. Neighbors make parking lots   **a.** into gardens.   **b.** into stores.

5. There are block parties   **a.** every summer.   **b.** every winter.

▶ *Show you understand*

How do these people help their neighborhoods? Write the correct letter next to each name.

___ **1.** George   **a.** plants community gardens.

_a_ **2.** Lillian   **b.** puts up a basketball net.

___ **3.** Cindy   **c.** builds benches.

___ **4.** Rosa   **d.** plants trees.

___ **5.** Sophie's family   **e.** has neighborhood watch meetings.

▶ *Talk more about it*

Think about these questions. Then ask and answer the questions with a partner.

> **1.** What do you like about your neighborhood?
>
> **2.** What do you want to change about your neighborhood?
>
> **3.** Do you know any community groups that help your neighborhood?

 Turn to *Remember the Words*, page 104.

TALK ABOUT IT

A. Look at the pictures. Read the questions. Mark (✗) the boxes in the chart. Talk about your answers with a partner.

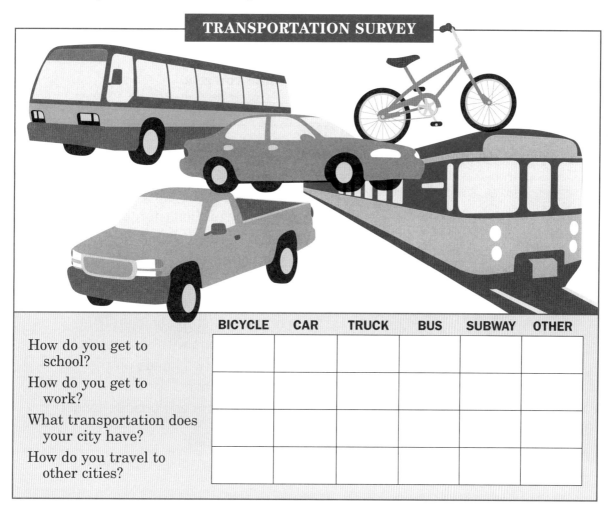

TRANSPORTATION SURVEY

	BICYCLE	CAR	TRUCK	BUS	SUBWAY	OTHER
How do you get to school?						
How do you get to work?						
What transportation does your city have?						
How do you travel to other cities?						

B. Think about these questions. Talk about your ideas with your partner.

1. Do you know how to drive?
2. Is a car necessary in your city? Why or why not?
3. Is it easy to learn how to drive? Why or why not?

Before You Read

Look at the picture. Look at the title of the reading. Guess the answers to the questions. Circle *a* or *b*.

1. What is this reading about? **a.** taking a driving test **b.** buying a new car
2. Who is driving the car? **a.** a test examiner **b.** a new driver

While You Read

Read this brochure. Think about your guesses while you read.

Get Behind the Wheel

Are you ready for your driving test? Read this brochure carefully.

Before the Test
Check your car. Does it have...
- gas in the gas tank?
- air in the tires?
- a horn, headlights, and windshield wipers that work?
- a rear license plate?

At the Test
It's important to be on time. Also, you have to arrive with another driver. Make sure you bring your learner's permit.

The examiner is going to test you on many things. Don't forget to...
- put on your seat belt <u>first</u>. Then put your key in the ignition.
- check your mirrors before you pull away from the curb.
- brake and stop completely at intersections with stop signs.
- drive with two hands on the steering wheel.
- signal before you change lanes.

After the Test
The examiner tells you your test results.
Did you fail? You can take the test again in two weeks.
Did you pass? Congratulations ! (It's OK to shake hands with your examiner!) Now you can get a temporary license. Welcome to the highways!

▶ What did you read?

Choose a different title for the reading. Circle _a_ or _b_.

a. Find a Driving School   **b.** Prepare for a Driving Test

▶ Read again

Read the sentences. Find three driving test mistakes. Mark (✗) them.

___ **1.** You arrive on time for the test.

___ **2.** You put your key in the ignition first. Then you put on your seat belt.

___ **3.** You check your mirrors first. Then you pull away from the curb.

___ **4.** You drive with one hand on the steering wheel.

___ **5.** You stop completely at intersections with a stop sign.

___ **6.** You signal after you change lanes.

▶ Show you understand

Complete this chart. Mark (✗) the correct boxes.

	BEFORE THE TEST	AT THE TEST	AFTER THE TEST
Bring your learner's permit.		✗	
Be on time.			
Put gas in the gas tank.			
Shake hands with the test examiner.			
Check the windshield wipers.			
Get your test results.			

▶ Talk more about it

Think about these questions. Talk about your ideas with a partner.

1. Why are driving tests necessary?

2. What mistakes do some new drivers make?

3. Are you a good driver? Why?

After You Read

▶ *Words, words, words*

Read these sentences. Fill in the blanks with the words in the box.

| horn | headlights | ignition | signal | tires | windshield wipers |

1. It's raining. Turn on your <u>windshield wipers</u> .
2. Be sure to put air in the _____.
3. Maybe he can't see you. Honk your _____.
4. This road is dark. Turn on your _____.
5. You can turn off the _____. The test is over.
6. You're changing lanes. Be sure to _____.

▶ *Puzzle: Mixed-up bumper stickers*

The words in each box make a sentence for the bumper sticker. Put the words in order. Write the sentence on the bumper sticker.

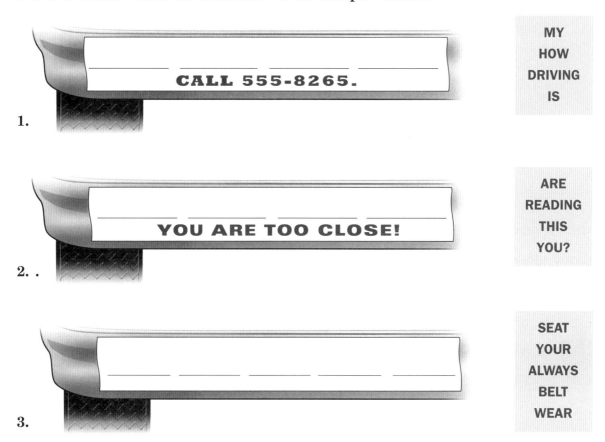

1.

_____ _____ _____ _____
CALL 555-8265.

MY
HOW
DRIVING
IS

2. .

_____ _____ _____ _____
YOU ARE TOO CLOSE!

ARE
READING
THIS
YOU?

3.

_____ _____ _____ _____ _____

SEAT
YOUR
ALWAYS
BELT
WEAR

READ MORE ABOUT IT

Before You Read

Look at the pictures. Look at the title of the reading. Guess the answers to the questions. Circle *a* or *b*.

1. Why is Jeff driving the car?

    a. to learn how to drive   **b.** to buy his first car

2. Where is Jeff driving?

    a. on a big highway   **b.** on a quiet road

While You Read

Read this story. Think about your guesses while you read.

Jeff's First Driving Lesson

Do you remember your first driving lesson? I do! This is my "first-time-behind-the-wheel" story.

My friend Dana is going to teach me. She drives to a quiet road away from the city.

She stops the car and turns off the ignition. She says, "OK, let's change places. You're the driver now."

I sit down and put on my seat belt. Then I turn on the ignition. I put both hands on the steering wheel. I'm very nervous. Dana says, "Now put your foot on the gas pedal." I do it, and the car moves forward slowly.

Soon we come to an intersection. I put my foot on the brake. The car stops. Dana

says, "Good job. Now turn to the right." I step on the gas and turn the steering wheel. The car turns quickly. But I keep the wheel in the "turn" position. The car keeps turning. And turning!

Dana screams, "Turn to the left! Put your foot on the brake." I hear her, but I can't do it. I'm too scared. My hands are "frozen" on the steering wheel. The car turns in a circle. It goes off the road and into a field of corn!

There's a farmer on a tractor nearby. Dana waves to him. She calls out, "Can you help us, please?" The man pulls our car out of the field with his tractor. I'm very embarrassed! But Dana just laughs.

▶ *Read again*

Are these sentences true? Circle *yes* or *no*.

1. Jeff remembers his first driving lesson.	yes	no
2. Dana drives to a busy street in the city.	yes	no
3. Jeff stops the car at the intersection.	yes	no
4. Jeff turns the steering wheel to the right.	yes	no
5. The car goes into a field of tomatoes.	yes	no
6. A farmer pulls their car out of the field with a truck.	yes	no

▶ *Show you understand*

Read the paragraph. Fill in the blanks with words from the box.

brake	seat belt	gas pedal	intersection	steering wheel

Jeff sits down in the driver's seat. He puts on his _____ _____. His friend
Dana says, "Now put your foot on the _____ _____." Soon they come to
an _____. Jeff stops the car and turns the _____ _____ to
the right. But he can't let go! The car starts to turn in a circle. Dana shouts, "Stop the car! Put
your foot on the _____."

▶ *Talk more about it*

Think about these questions. Then ask and answer the questions with a partner.

> **1.** Jeff's driving teacher is his friend. Is this a good idea?
>
> **2.** Do you remember your first driving lesson? Describe it.

 Turn to *Remember the Words*, page 104.

Unit 11
Working Families

TALK ABOUT IT

A. Work with a small group. Look at the pictures of different families at work. Talk about the family relationships and their occupations.

B. Think about these questions. Talk about your ideas with your group.

> **1.** What are the good things about families working together?
>
> **2.** What problems do working families have?

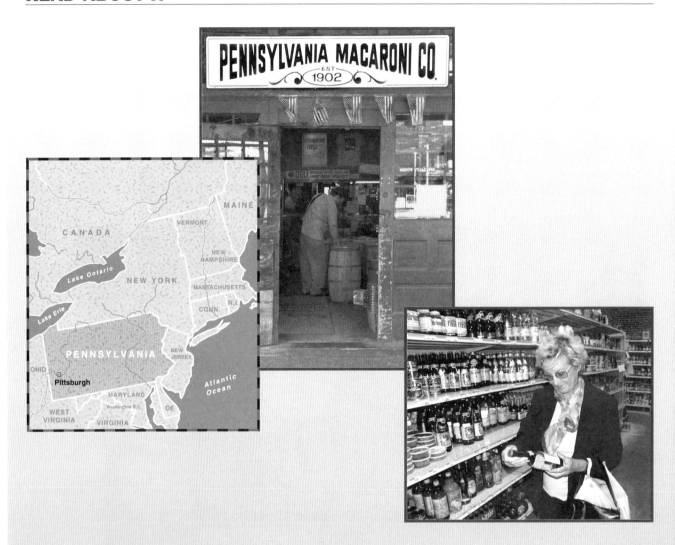

Before You Read

Look at the pictures. Look at the title of the reading. Guess the answers to the questions.

1. What kind of business is the Pennsylvania Macaroni Company?

   a. a very big company   **b.** a family business

2. How old is the Pennsylvania Macaroni Company?

   a. more than 50 years old   **b.** less than 10 years old

While You Read

Read this newspaper article. Think about your guesses while you read.

A Business with a History

The Pennsylvania Macaroni Company is a family business. The company makes pasta. They also sell olive oil, cheese, and many other food products. Here is a short history of the company.

1902

The Sunseri brothers, Augustino, Salvatore, and Michael, come to the United States from Italy. The brothers want to start a business. They love pasta, and they know how to make it! They open the Pennsylvania Macaroni Company in Pittsburgh, Pennsylvania.

1910

There is a big fire at the factory. The Sunseri brothers and their families are very sad! They still want their business. They build a new factory!

1940

Now Augustino's sons are working at the factory. They are good businessmen. They still sell pasta, but now they sell olive oil, cheese, and other Italian products, too. The company is very successful. They sell 200,000 pounds of cheese every week.

Today, Jimmy and Nino, Augustino's grandsons, oversee the family business. They start work very early in the morning. The factory workers start early, too. They put pasta, olive oil, and cheese in the delivery trucks. The truck drivers deliver the food to many restaurants and supermarkets in Pittsburgh.

There is also a market at the factory. The market is famous. People love the market. Jimmy and Nino are always there. They love their work. Visit them any time!

▶ *What did you read?*

What is the reading about? Circle *a* or *b*.

a. a family food factory and market   **b.** Italian food in Pittsburgh, Pennsylvania

▶ *Read again*

Complete the answers to these questions.

1. Where are Augustino, Salvatore, and Michael Sunseri from?

They are from _____.

2. What kind of business do the three brothers start?

They start a _____.

3. Where is their business?

Their business is in _____.

4. What happens to the business in 1910?

There is a big _____.

5. What are three things the Sunseri business sells today?

It sells _____, _____, and _____.

▶ *Show you understand*

Put the sentences in the correct order. Number them from 1–5.

____ The Sunseri factory burns in a fire.

_1_ Augustino, Salvatore, and Michael Sunseri come to the United States.

____ Jimmy and Nino Sunseri are working at the family business.

____ The three Sunseri brothers start a pasta factory.

____ Augustino Sunseri's sons start selling olive oil and cheese.

▶ *Talk more about it*

Think about these questions. Then ask and answer the questions with a partner.

> **1.** Do you want to start a family business? Why or why not?
>
> **2.** Do you know about a family business? What kind of business is it? Tell about it.

After You Read

▶ *Words, words, words*

Read the sentences. What do the underlined words mean? Circle *a* or *b*.

1. The Sunseri Brothers open a <u>pasta</u> factory.

    a. cheese   **b.** macaroni

2. Everyone likes the Sunseris' products. Their business is <u>successful</u>.

    a. good   **b.** bad

3. The grandsons <u>oversee</u> the family business.

    a. watch over   **b.** start

4. Jimmy and Nino are at the <u>company</u> every day.

    a. business   **b.** family home

5. The business is very old. This is the <u>history</u> of the business.

    a. a story from the past   **b.** a story that isn't true

▶ *Write*

Write about your favorite store. Answer these questions. Write your answers in paragraph form. Use the lines below.

What is the name of the store?

What does it sell?

What do you usually buy there?

Why do you go to this store?

> I shop at Hassan's Grocery. It sells food. I usually buy meat and vegetables at Hassan's Grocery. It is clean, and the people are friendly.

_____

_____

_____

_____

_____

_____

_____

A day-care center

"Mom" at home

Before You Read

Look at the pictures. Look at the title of the reading. Guess the answers to the questions. Circle *a* or *b*.

1. What are the letters about?

    a. work and family   **b.** finding a job

2. What does "Working Mom" do?

    a. She works at home.   **b.** She takes her child to a
                                    day-care center.

While You Read

Read the letters. Are your guesses correct?

Need Advice? Ask Alice...

Today's topic: Working Moms

Dear Alice,

I need some help. I have a great job. I'm a computer programmer. The people in my office are great, and my work is interesting. But I have a two-year-old daughter. She goes to a day-care center now. It's a good day-care center.

Sometimes I think about leaving my job and staying at home with my daughter. I want to spend more time with her. But there is a problem. We really need the money. My husband is working, but he doesn't make a lot of money. Do you have any advice?

—Working Mom

Dear Working Mom,

Many mothers have the same problem. Your situation is not unusual. There is no easy answer, but here are some ideas.

You like your job. Talk to your boss. Maybe you can work from home or work part-time. A lot of computer programmers do this. Maybe you can, too.

Should you quit? I don't know. Many families have difficulties because of money. Think carefully before you quit your job. Only you can decide what is right for you.

You'll make the right choice!

—Alice

▶ Read again

Read these sentences. Which sentences are correct? Circle *a* or *b*.

1. a. Working Mom doesn't like her job. **b.** Working Mom likes her job.

2. a. Working Mom has one child. **b.** Working Mom has two children.

3. a. Working Mom's husband is working. **b.** Working Mom's husband isn't working.

4. a. Alice tells Working Mom to quit. **b.** Alice says Working Mom needs to think about it.

5. a. Working Mom needs the money from her job. **b.** Working Mom doesn't need a job.

▶ Write

What should Working Mom do? Answer the questions. Use your answers to complete the letter.

1. Should Working Mom quit her job? _____

2. Why? _____

> Dear Working Mom,
>
> I think you (should / shouldn't) quit your job. _____
>
> _____
>
> _____
>
> _____
>
> _____ (Your name)

▶ Talk more about it

Think about these questions. Talk about your answers with a partner.

> **1.** What are good things about day-care centers? What are some problems with day-care centers?
>
> **2.** Your friend works. She doesn't want to use a day-care center for her daughter. What can she do?

 Turn to *Remember the Words*, page 104.

TALK ABOUT IT

A. Where do people usually do these activities? Mark (✗) the boxes in the chart. Talk about your answers with a partner.

Activity	INDOORS	OUTDOORS	BOTH
Skiing			
Hiking			
Going to the movies			
Camping			
Playing baseball			
Playing an instrument			
Watching TV			
Running			

B. Think about these questions. Then ask and answer the questions with your partner.

1. Which activities in the chart do you do? Where do you do them?
2. What other sports and leisure activities do you like?

READ ABOUT IT

Before You Read

Look at the picture. Look at the title of the reading. Guess the answers
to the questions. Circle *a* or *b*.

1. What is the person doing?   **a.** skiing   **b.** watching a movie about skiing
2. Where is this happening?   **a.** outdoors   **b.** indoors

While You Read

Read this magazine article. Think about your guesses while you read.

No Snow? No Problem!

Sometimes sports are like weather. They change with the seasons. People like to play basketball or baseball outdoors on warm spring days. They like to go swimming in hot summer weather. People can enjoy some sports all year round. In the winter, they can swim and play basketball indoors. They can run in cold weather.

But what about skiing? Most people think skiing is only a winter activity. For many years, skiing was only a winter activity. But this isn't true anymore. Now there are "snowdomes." Snowdomes are big buildings. There is snow in the building. Now people can go skiing in the summer—indoors! People can also go skiing in warm places where it never snows.

There are about 30 snowdomes in the world. There are no snowdomes in the United States at this time, but there are plans for snowdomes in Los Angeles, Las Vegas, and Miami. All of these cities are in warm places. There's no snow, and there are no mountains!

Snowdomes also have other activities. Some of them have swimming pools or rock climbing walls. Is the snowdome the gym of the future? Probably not. Skiing in a snowdome can be expensive. It can cost about $50 a day or more to ski in a snowdome. You can see five movies for that price!

▶ *What did you read?*

What is the reading about? Circle the best answer.

a. Snowdomes are very large buildings.

b. People can ski in the summer in a snowdome.

c. Skiing is often an expensive sport.

▶ *Read again*

Complete the answers to these questions.

1. What is the main activity in a snowdome?   The main activity is _____.

2. How many snowdomes are there in the world?   There are about _____ snowdomes.

3. How much does skiing in a snowdome cost?   It costs about _____ for one day.

4. How many snowdomes are there in the United States now?   There are _____ snowdomes in the United States now.

▶ *Show you understand*

Read this paragraph. Fill in the blanks with words from the box.

skiing	snow	indoors	movies	swimming pools

In a snowdome, people can go _____ in the summer. Snowdomes have _____ inside. People can ski _____. Skiing isn't the only activity in a snowdome. Some snowdomes have _____. It costs about $50 to go skiing in a snowdome. You can see about five _____ for the same price!

▶ *Talk more about it*

Think about these questions. Talk about your ideas with a partner.

> **1.** Are snowdomes a good idea? Why or why not?
>
> **2.** What sports do you play (or watch) in the summer? In the winter?
>
> **3.** Do you play (or watch) the same sports in summer and winter?

After You Read

► *Word forms: verb + -ing*

**Complete the chart with the simple form or the *-ing* form of the verb.
You can find the words in the reading.**

SIMPLE FORM	-ing FORM
	swimming
run	
climb	
	playing
ski	

Which forms have double letters? _____

► *Write*

**Write about your favorite sport. Answer these questions. Write your
answers in paragraph form. Use the lines below.**

What is your favorite sport?

Do you play this sport or watch it?

Where do you play (or watch) this sport?

When do you play (or watch) this sport?

I live _____

_____

_____

_____

_____

_____

_____

_____

*Soccer is my
favorite sport.
I play soccer, and
I watch it on TV.
I play soccer in the
park. I play on the
weekends.*

READ MORE ABOUT IT

Before You Read

Scan the brochure for the holidays. Mark (X) them.

scan = look quickly to find specific information

_X_ Thanksgiving   ___ Halloween

___ New Year's Day   ___ Valentine's Day

___ Memorial Day   ___ Fourth of July

___ Labor Day

While You Read

Read the brochure. Check your answers while you read.

Fit for the Holidays

You can lose that extra holiday weight!

It always starts the same way…

You have a big meal at Thanksgiving. During the winter holidays, everyone gives you cookies and candy. In January, you look in the mirror and say, "I need to lose some weight!"

Does this sound like you?

Come to the Greenfield Community Center and get in shape! You don't need to join an expensive gym. Your community center can meet all your exercise needs!

Start today!

Go swimming three times a week in our indoor pool. You'll feel good by Valentine's Day!

Try running! You can go running with our community fitness experts! You'll walk at the front of the parade on Memorial Day.

Try basketball or tennis on the community courts. You'll look good when you watch the fireworks on the Fourth of July!

Does this sound like fun? It is! And, you'll meet people and make friends.

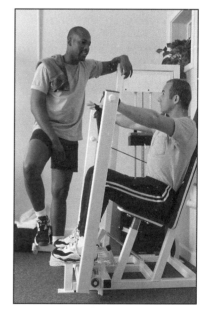

Call or visit the Greenfield Community Center to learn more about our programs.

Greenfield Community Center
1001 Cedar Boulevard
555-9724
Open from 7 a.m. – 9 p.m.
Monday – Saturday

▶ *What did you read?*

What is the reading about? Circle *a* or *b*.

a. community activities for the holidays

b. exercise programs at the community center

▶ *Read again*

Read the sentences. Circle *yes* or *no*.

1.	Some people eat too much during the winter holidays.	yes	no
2.	The Greenfield Community Center is an expensive gym.	yes	no
3.	There is a pool at the Greenfield Community Center.	yes	no
4.	These exercise programs are a good way to meet people.	yes	no

▶ *Show you understand*

Which exercise programs does the Greenfield Community Center have? Mark (✗) them.

___ **1.** swimming

___ **2.** running

___ **3.** baseball

___ **4.** basketball

___ **5.** tennis

___ **6.** soccer

▶ *Talk more about it*

Think about these questions. Talk about your ideas with a partner.

1. Are exercise classes a good place to meet people? Why or why not?

2. Is there a community center in your neighborhood? What activities does it offer?

 Turn to *Remember the Words*, page 104.

TEACHER'S NOTES

Teaching the Units

There are three main sections in each unit. TALK ABOUT IT introduces the topic and activates students' prior knowledge. READ ABOUT IT and READ MORE ABOUT IT each contain the components of an effective reading lesson: pre-reading, reading, and post-reading activities.

Before You Read

Teachers can make these pre-reading activities most effective by initially leading the students through them, thereby modeling the strategies a competent reader uses prior to reading a text. The strategies are repeated and reinforced as students progress through the book.

New vocabulary is most effectively presented in context. In *Read All About It Starter*, many new vocabulary words are evident in the picture captions or the *Before You Read* questions. To help students guess the meaning of the words, the teacher can point out any clues in the captions, questions, or pictures that may inform the student's guessing. Modeling this approach to guessing meaning from context is an effective way to accustom students to using the strategy themselves. To avoid over-whelming the students, working with a maximum of about eight new words is recommended.

New words are often reviewed in the *After You Read* section of each unit. When students encounter words they want to learn, they can record them in their personal vocabulary diary, Remember the Words on page 104.

Each reading incorporates a number of words from the corresponding unit and other units of *The Basic Oxford Picture Dictionary*, so the readings can be used to reinforce that vocabulary. See page 00 for the Word List with references to *The Basic Oxford Picture Dictionary*.

While You Read

Since reading is most often a solitary activity, silent reading is an important part of the learning process. Therefore, the readings in this text are meant to be read individually and silently first. Once students

have worked thoroughly with the reading and follow-up exercises, the teacher or students may read the passage aloud to work on pronunciation and to develop fluency in oral reading. The accompanying audiotape can also be used at this time.

Students should be encouraged to guess the meaning of unknown words from context or skip over them just as competent readers do. Teachers should point out to students that they will usually be able to grasp the main ideas of the readings and answer the comprehension questions without understanding every word. They should read for general meaning the first time and refer back to the reading for details during the *Read again* exercises.

The teacher may want to set a short time limit for students to read the passage in the *While You Read* section, and to answer the questions in *What did you read?* and *Read again*. A time limit encourages students to rely on context clues for meaning. It also allows all the students to finish reading and answering the first set of questions simultaneously, so that they can begin pair or group work at the same time.

Although reading the passage and doing the *Read Again* exercises are intended to be done individually, the rest of the activities in *While You Read* can be done in pairs or small groups. Working together gives students the opportunity to negotiate the meaning of the readings and to develop communication skills. During group work, it is helpful to give students a time limit to complete the work, and to assign student roles, such as discussion leader, recorder, reporter, or timekeeper to help the groups run smoothly. Frequently changing pairings or groupings gives students the experience of listening and talking to a variety of speakers.

While communication skills are an important part of the learning process, all exercises can be completed individually if necessary, and most answers can be found in the Answer Key starting on page 89.

After You Read

In this section, reading skills are reinforced through vocabulary and writing activities. These activities can be done individually in class or used for homework or assessment purposes.

READ MORE ABOUT IT
Since READ MORE ABOUT IT will probably take place in a new class period, teachers may want to conduct a review discussion of the topic. They can rely on students who read the first passage for answers to specific review questions. More general questions can be answered by those who did not read the first passage. In this way, all students can benefit from the discussion.

Time Frame

Read All About It Starter is easily adaptable to different class situations. Activities can be done in a relatively short period of time or exploited to the fullest extent, depending on the needs and goals of the students and the time available. In a TALK ABOUT IT section, for example, a teacher could lead students through the activities to shorten the time or have them work in small groups to lengthen it. Teachers can omit activities that do not suit their objectives.

Units can be easily divided to span more than one class period. In one class, students can complete TALK ABOUT IT through *Talk more about it* for the first reading. *After You Read* can be done for homework. READ MORE ABOUT IT can be reserved for another class period.

Unit-by-Unit Notes

The following notes provide information and ideas for both new and experienced teachers.
Procedural Notes (PRO) offer ideas for specific lesson plans and classroom management.
Extension Activities (EXT) are additional reading, writing, or discussion tasks in which students can apply the skills they have learned.
Word Families (WF) identify important relationships among word meaning, form, and use. Have students scan the reading for the words and read the sentences where they find them. Then have them use the words in oral or written sentences.

Unit 1 Weather Watch

Page 1, Extra! Extra!

The first TV weather report was broadcast on October 14, 1941, on station WNBT in New York City.

How's the Weather?

How's the Weather? discusses some old ideas and sayings about weather. Some of these are based on observation of the behavior and appearance of animals. Others depend on looking at the stars, the planets, cloud formations, or colors in the sky.

Page 3, While You Read

WF: *n.* rain   *adj.* rainy   *n.* sun   *adj.* sunny
n. sky   *n.* skies

Page 4, Talk more about it

EXT: Introduce students to this well-known weather rhyme.

Red sky at night, sailors delight.
Red sky in the morning, sailors take warning.

Page 5, Puzzle: A secret word

PRO: If students have difficulty getting started with the puzzle, tell them that the first letter of each word is in the correct position.

The Groundhog Weather Report

Groundhog Day, February 2, is the only holiday in the United States named after an animal. An old legend says that if a groundhog comes out of its burrow on February 2 and sees its shadow, winter will last for six more weeks. If the groundhog does not see its shadow, spring will come soon.

The most famous groundhog celebration in the U.S. is in the small town of Punxsutawney, Pennsylvania. Every year, thousands of people gather to await the emergence of the "official weather forecaster," Groundhog Phil.
(Another name for the groundhog is woodchuck.)

Page 8, While You Read

PRO: Have students look at the pictures and the captions. Then have them find the part of the reading that each one refers to.

Page 8, Write

PRO: In this activity, students write a weather report based on a picture. Have students look at the picture. Then brainstorm some vocabulary with the class. Have students look at the picture of the thermometer on the page, or you could bring a real thermometer to the class. Point out that the U.S. usually uses the Fahrenheit scale for reporting temperatures, while other countries use the Celsius (centigrade) scale. Call out temperatures (*It's 85 degrees today*) and have students respond with *hot, warm, cool* or *cold*. Then have them work individually to complete the weather report.

EXT: Have students find another "weather" picture in a newspaper or magazine and then write a weather report about it.

UNIT 2 Up and Down Days

Page 9, Talk About It

PRO: Introduce the idea of talking about daily schedules by doing a quick class survey to find out which students are "early birds" and which are "night owls." Ask questions such as: What time do you usually get up/go to bed? What time of day do you like best, the morning or the evening?

Life Above Ground

Page 11, While You Read

Life Above Ground is based on a true story. On December 10, 1977, a 23-year-old woman named Julia Hill climbed into a centuries-old California redwood tree in order to save it from loggers. Julia named the tree "Luna." She became a celebrity, speaking to reporters around the world via cellular phone and writing newspaper and magazine articles. Julia Hill is the founder of the Circle of Life Foundation, which encourages people to "live in a way that honors the diversity and interdependence of all life."

Julia Hill was given the nickname "Butterfly" when she was seven years old. Her family was hiking, and a butterfly landed on Julia's shoulder and rested there. Many people refer to Julia as "Julia Butterfly."

EXT: Ask students: Do you have a nickname? / How did you get it?

Page 13, Word search puzzle

PRO: The words in the puzzle go across, down, and diagonally. None of the words is upside down or backwards.

Page 13, Write

PRO: Go over the example in the letter with the students, the phrase *combs her hair*. Point out that when they use the phrase in this sentence, *comb* changes to *combs* after the singular pronoun *she*. Then have students fill in the blanks in the first sentence. Make sure they add the *–s* to *get* in *gets dressed*.

Life Below Ground

Page 14, Read More About It

PRO: Have students go over the subway map. Looking from top to bottom, have them identify the first and last stops on the number 9 line, Van Cortlandt Park and South Ferry.

Page 15, While You Read

WF: *v.* goes   *v.* going   *v.* get   *v.* gets

PRO: After students have read the article, have them look at the illustration and find the section of the story that it relates to.

Page 16, Scan for numbers

PRO: Scan—Model the activity. Show students how to run their fingers down the reading to search for the numbers. Give them about two minutes to complete the exercise.

Page 16, Talk more about it

EXT: Have students compare their answers to the *Talk more about it* questions as a class. Who has an unusual schedule or works in an unusual or interesting environment?

Unit 3 HiTech Families

Page 17, Talk About It

PRO: You can use the picture to present the word *twins*, pointing out the two girls at the bottom of the picture. This will be useful in the reading on page 18, where Teresa's mother has twins.

Teresa's Web Page

Page 18, While You Read

Teresa's Web Page is representative of a Web log or *blog*. Blogs are online diaries or journals that are accessible to the journal keeper's friends and family as well as the general public. You may want to do some quick searches on your own for blogs and share these authentic blogs with students.

EXT: Ask students the following questions: Do you write in a diary or a journal? Is it a good idea to do this? Why or why not? Do you allow others to read your diary or journal?

Do you write a blog? Do you know anyone who does?

Page 19, Read again

EXT: Ask students to write correct sentences for the untrue sentences.

Page 19, Show you understand

EXT: Ask students to write the sentences in order on a separate piece of paper.

Computer Talk

Page 21, While You Read

EXT: The "person on the street" interview is a common occurrence in many countries. Basically, a reporter asks many people to answer the same question. Ask students if they know of any television shows, newspapers, or magazines that use the "person on the street" format.

Unit 4 Homes on the Edge

A Yurt: A Home to Go

Page 24, While You Read

PRO: Point out that many of the parts of the tree house from the preceding page are visible in these photographs. Elicit the parts of the yurt that students can name.

EXT: To aid comprehension of the words for some of the tools mentioned in the article, show students the real tools, e.g., a tape measure, a screwdriver, etc.

Page 25, Show you understand

EXT: Ask students to write the sentences in order on a separate piece of paper.

At Home on a Houseboat

Page 27, While You Read

EXT: Ask students: What are the features of your neighborhood or home?
What is good or bad about living in a houseboat?

UNIT 5 Shop Smart

Page 29, Talk About It

PRO: Review food vocabulary using visuals, realia, or actual food items.

EXT: You could introduce this page by having students play a Vocabulary Food Bee. Divide the class into two teams. Call out one of the three categories in the picture: Fruits and Vegetables, Dairy Products, or Meat and Seafood. Students from each team take turns naming one food in that category. Award points for each correct answer. The team with the most points wins.

Smart Supermarket Shopping

Page 30, While You Read

WF: *v.* shop   *v.* shopping   *v.* go shopping
n. shopper

Page 30, Extra! Extra!

Supermarket shopping carts last about 10 years. During that time, the wheels are replaced, on the average, three times.

Page 32, Write

EXT: Make a Shopping List

1. Have students form small groups. Assign one student to record the group information. Give students about 5–10 minutes to create a shopping list for a class party. Call time and have one student from each group read the list. Combine the responses to create one class shopping list on the board.
2. Bring in supermarket circulars or flyers. Distribute some to each group and have students search for items that are on their shopping list.

Page 32, Supermarket Tic-Tac-Toe

PRO: Students can mark boxes with the traditional "X" or "O," or they could put their initials in the boxes they win. The first person to get three in a row—up, down, or diagonal—wins the game. As far as possible, let students work on their own to decide if sentences are correct or not, helping only as needed.

Read for Your Health!

Page 34, Scan for numbers

PRO: Scan—Model the activity. Show students how to run their fingers down the reading to search for the numbers. Give them about 2 minutes to complete the exercise.

EXT: Use real food packages and labels and have students compare similar brands, for example, regular and reduced fat potato chips. They can use the language in this section as a model for conversation.

Page 34, Talk more about it

EXT: As a follow-up, have students write a simple "food diary" of what they eat in a 24-hour period. The next day, have them share their food diaries and identify one change they would like to make.

UNIT 6 Let's Eat Out

Page 35, Talk About It

EXT: Have students brainstorm other possible survey questions. For example, they might ask about popular eating places in their area. Write the questions on the board for students to answer. Then tabulate the results for the whole class.

Norma's Restaurant Review

Page 36, While You Read

PRO: Ask students about restaurant reviews. Do they ever read restaurant reviews in newspapers or magazines? Bring a couple of sample reviews to class, if possible for restaurants they might know about.

Page 37, Show you understand

EXT: Have students brainstorm other words for the categories in the chart and add them to the list.

Breakfast at Nat's

Page 39, While You Read

EXT: Have students brainstorm additional items to add to the three menu categories: main courses, side orders, and beverages.

EXT: Bring in some sample breakfast menus and have students practice asking and answering questions. Model questions that both a waitress and customers might ask. Students can take turns practicing a simple dialog: *Are you ready to order? What's in the Breakfast Burrito?*

Page 40, Show you understand

EXT: Talking About Prices. After students complete the activity, review the different ways of saying monetary amounts. $5.25: *Five dollars and twenty-five cents* or *Five twenty-five.*

Unit 7 Working Clothes

Art Student to Fashion Designer

Page 42, Before You Read

PRO: Ask students to cover the reading text before they make their guesses. You could ask them the reasons for their guesses, but don't tell them the answers at this time. Let them discover this as they read. Students should not feel they have made a "mistake" if some of their guesses are wrong. The purpose of the activity is for students to learn to think about words that *might* be in a reading.

Page 42, While You Read

WF: *v.* design   *n.* designer

EXT: Ask students: Do you know anybody who has turned his or her hobby into a career? Tell about the person.

EXT: Ask students to mention the names of other clothes items they know.

Page 44, Write

PRO: You could have students write their paragraphs on a separate piece of paper or in their notebooks. Make sure they write the sentences as a paragraph and not as a list.

Free Work Clothes

Page 45, While You Read

Students may not know that in the United States there are stores that accept donations of used clothes to sell or give to people who need them.

Back on Track Workwear also depends on donations, but it is very selective about the quality of clothing it accepts. It also has ways of making sure that customers are not giving untrue information about themselves or their work situation.

Page 46, Words, words, words

EXT: Have students compare answers as a whole class.

Unit 8 Call the Doctor

Page 47, Talk About It

PRO: Have students look at the pictures and say what they can see in each of the three places.

EXT: Ask students: Where do you go in an emergency? Do you prefer to go to a doctor's private clinic (office) or to the hospital? Why?

The Barter Clinic

Page 48, While You Read

EXT: Ask students: What do you think of Dr. Osborne's unusual way of practicing medicine? Do you know anybody who practices his or her career in an unusual way? Tell about the person. Imagine you are ill. Would you visit a doctor like Dr. Osborne? Why / Why not?

What Doctors Ask

Page 51, While You Read

EXT: Ask students: Can you think of any other questions doctors ask patients? Why are doctors' questions important?

UNIT 9 Community Spirit

A Trip on Route 66

The planning, development, and ultimate demise of Route 66 is an important story in the history of the United States. From its start in 1926, public road planners envisioned U.S. Route 66 as a way to connect the main streets of rural and urban communities. At that time, most small towns were not near any major roads. Transport of most products took place by train.

Route 66 played an important part in the many changes in American life, including the rise of the trucking industry, and the evolution of "tourist" facilities such as motels, roadside restaurants, and service stations. By the 1970s, nearly all parts of Route 66 were replaced by faster four-lane highways. Route 66 was officially "de-commissioned" in 1984.

About 85 per cent of the original road is still drivable, and tourists from around the world visit "America's Main Street" each year.

Page 53, While You Read

PRO:
1. Check to make sure students know what a journal is. Ask if any of them ever write in journals of any kind, to record special events like trips or day-to-day activities.
2. Point out that spelling *Standin'* in the name *Standin' on the Corner Park* is an informal spelling used to reflect the way people often say *–ing* words in conversation.
3. Students may notice a difference between the sum of the two numbers on the sign for Adrian, Texas ($1139 \times 2 = 2278$) and the figure of "about $2,400''$" given in the text for the length of Route 66. Explain that the number 2,4000 is an approximate length. The exact length is impossible to determine because of changes in the road since it "closed" in 1984.

Page 56, Talk more about it

EXT: Bring in brochures from travel agencies or photos of vacation destinations. Ask students: Which places would you like to visit? How would you get there?

EXT: Pack Your Bags. Divide students into groups. Have them brainstorm a list of 10 items they would pack for a bus trip along Route 66. One student can record the group responses, while another can report to the class. What are the most popular items?

Page 57, Scan for numbers

PRO: Scan—Model the activity. Show students how to run their fingers down the reading to search for the numbers. Give them about 2–3 minutes to complete the exercise.

Neighbor to Neighbor

Page 59, While You Read

WF: *n.* community   *n.* communities   *n.* family
n. families   *n.* neighbors   *n.* neighborhood
v. clean up   *adj.* clean

PRO: Have students look at the pictures and talk about what is happening. Have student pairs brainstorm words that they know about the pictures. After they read the article, have them check their list for words that appear in the reading.

Page 60, Read again

EXT: Have students copy the first part of each sentence and write an alternate ending.
Model the first sentence as an example:1. In a great community, <u>people have fun together</u>.

Page 60, Talk more about it

EXT: Have students talk about their community. Discuss problems and solutions from their own experience.

UNIT 10 Behind the Wheel

Page 61, Talk About It

EXT: Have students talk about transportation problems and solutions in their community.
To generate discussion, first provide some statements where students can respond with *yes/no* cards or a show of hands. Sample answers: *There are too many cars on the road. People drive too fast here. The bus is always late.*

Get Behind the Wheel

Page 62, While You Read

PRO: There are three compound nouns in this reading. Give students one as an example. Then ask them to find the two others. (They are *windshield*, *headlights*, and *highway*.) You could also ask students to find the expressions *gas tank*, *steering wheel*, *license plate*, *stop sign*, and *seat belt*.

Page 63, Read again

EXT: Have students correct the sentences that contain a driving mistake.

Page 64, Puzzle: Mixed-up bumper stickers

EXT: Have students talk about other bumper stickers they have seen on vehicles. If they can't

think of any, ask them to look for examples and write them down for the next class.

Jeff's First Driving Lesson

Page 65, While You Read

EXT: Review Jeff's driving story. Have students change the story to third person. They should identify the sentences that start with "I" and rewrite them. For example, *I put my foot on the brake. > <u>He puts</u> his foot on the brake.*

Page 66, Read again

EXT: Have students correct the sentences that are not true.

Unit 11 Working Families

Page 67, Talk About It

PRO: Before students begin to work in groups, brainstorm a few questions they can ask about the pictures: Where are the people? What are they doing? What can you see in the picture? etc.

The Pennsylvania Macaroni Factory

Page 68, Read About It

PRO: Go over the map with the students. Show them a map of the whole United States to identify the location of Pennsylvania.

Page 69, While You Read

PRO: Point out the timeline in the middle of the reading. This gives a brief history of the business.

Page 70, Show you understand

EXT: Ask students to write the sentences in order on a separate piece of paper.

Page 70, Talk more about it

EXT: If a lot of students say they would like to start a family business (or are already involved in one), have them talk about this with whole class. What kinds of businesses are the people in the class interested in?

Working Moms

Page 73, While You Read

WF: *v.* work   *n.* work   *adj.* working

PRO: Point out that many newspapers and magazines have advice columns. Readers can send letters explaining their problems and get answers or advice from the editor or a specialist.

Point out also that day-care centers are places that provide care for babies and young children during the day while parents are working.

EXT: Ask students: Are there people in your community who work from home? What kinds of jobs do they have? Is working from home a good idea? Why or why not?

Page 74, Talk more about it

EXT: In small groups, students discuss the following question: Should working mothers quit their jobs? Why or why not?

Unit 12 Keeping Fit

Page 76, While You Read

No Snow? No Problem!

EXT: Ask students: What sports can you play all year long? How is this possible?

Page 78, Word forms: verb + *-ing*

PRO: The spellings of the *–ing* form can be challenging for students. Point out that there are rules for adding the *–ing* suffix.
1. Words ending in one consonant preceded by one vowel: double the final consonant before adding *–ing*.
2. Words ending in *y* or more than one consonant: add *–ing*
3. Words ending in *e* preceded by a consonant: drop the e and add *–ing*
Point out the double *i* in the word *skiing*. In this case, the double letter is simply a coincidence as the word *ski* ends with the letter *i*.

Fit for the Holidays

Page 79, While You Read

Some students may not be familiar with all the United States holidays mentioned in the reading.

Thanksgiving—This is a national holiday that is always the fourth Thursday in November. People typically gather with family and friends to share a meal of turkey, mashed potatoes, pumpkin pie, and many other traditional foods. The holiday commemorates a meal in which the early colonists gave thanks for their first harvest.

Valentine's Day—This day celebrates romance and love. Valentine's Day is always celebrated on February 14.

Memorial Day—This national holiday honors those who died in military service of the United States. Many communities have a parade for this holiday. It is observed the last Monday of May, but is traditionally celebrated May 30.

Fourth of July—This national holiday celebrates the independence of the United States from England. It is typically celebrated with fireworks and parades.

EXT: Ask students: What are some interesting things that happen on national holidays in other countries? What traditional foods do people eat for these holidays?

ANSWER KEY

Unit 1

Talk About It [page 1]

The weather outside	TV weather report	
	Same	Different
It's windy		X
It's cloudy		X
It's raining		X
It's 68 degrees	X	

Before You Read [page 2]

a

How's the Weather?

What did you read? [page 4]

b

Read again [page 4]

1. c   2. d   3. e   4. a   5. b

Show you understand [page 4]

Colors	Times of Day	Things in the sky	Weather
white	evening	moon	snow
red	night	stars	rain, rainy
gray	tomorrow	sun	sunny
blue	morning		cloudy
			cold

Words, words, words [page 5]

1. tomorrow   2. snow   3. cloudy
4. stars   5. morning

Puzzle: A secret word [page 5]

RED
TODAY
MORNING
BLUE
TOMORROW
NIGHT
WHITE
Secret Word: WEATHER

The Groundhog Weather Report

Before You Read [page 6]

1. b   2. a

Read again [page 8]

1. a   2. b   3. a   4. b   5. b

Write [page 8]

Possible answer: rainy and cloudy, 45°, cool

Unit 2

Talk About It [page 9]

Who…	Joseph	J.J.
gets up at 10 a.m.?		X
works at the store in the morning?	X	
eats dinner at 5:45?	X	X
goes to the university in the evening?		X
goes to bed early?	X	

What do Joseph and J.J. do together?

Answer: They eat dinner together.

Before You Read [page 10]

1. b   2. b

Life Above Ground

What did you read? [page 12]

b

Read again [page 12]

1. a   2. a.   3. b   4. a   5. b

Show you understand [page 12]

4 She reads letters.
1 Julia gets up early.
6 She goes to sleep.
5 She talks on her cell phone.
3 She cooks breakfast.
2 She gets dressed.

Word search puzzle [page 13]

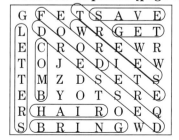

Write [page 13]

	A	B
1.	comb	hair
2.	get	dressed
3.	write	letters
4.	bring	food
5.	save	trees

Life Below Ground

Before You Read [page 14]

1. a   2. a

What did you read? [page 16]

b

Read again [page 16]

1. b   2. b   3. a   4. b   5. a

Scan for numbers [page 16]

1. 4:30 a.m.   2. 5:30 a.m.   3. 7:50 a.m.
4. 8:26 a.m.   5. 1:45 p.m.

Unit 3

Teresa's Web Page

Before You Read? [page 18]

1. a   2. b

What did you read? [page 19]

a

Read again [page 19]

1. no   2. yes   3. yes   4. no   5. no

Show you understand [page 19]

4   The twins are born.
5   Teresa graduates from high school.
2   The Salvo-Duarte family moves to the
    United States.
3   Teresa starts school in San Diego.
1   Teresa's father gets a job in San Diego.

Words, words, words [page 20]

1. b   2. e   3. a   4. c   5. d

Computer Talk

Before You Read [page 21]

1. b   2. a

Read again [page 22]

X 5. mail packages at the post office

Show you understand [page 22]

1. Regina   2. Sara   3. Carlos   4. Oleg

Unit 4

Talk About It [page 23]

TK
TK
TK
TK
TK

A Yurt: A Home to Go

Before You Read [page 24]

1. yes   2. no

What did you read? [page 25]

a

Read again [page 25]

1. a   2. a   3. b   4. b   5. b

Show you understand [page 25]

5   Move into the yurt.
1   Make the yurt's floor.
3   Put the roof on.
4   Put the deck on the front of the yurt.
2   Put up the walls and door.

Words, words, words [page 26]

1. tape measure
2. floor
3. tent
4. hammer
5. cloth

At Home on a Houseboat

Before You Read [page 27]

b

What did you read? [page 28]

Life on a houseboat is good.
or
Life is good on a houseboat.

Read again [page 28]

1. yes   2. no   3. no   4. yes   5. no

Show you understand [page 28]

1. bedrooms
2. bathroom
3. kitchen
4. living room
5. houseboats

Unit 5

Talk About It [page 29]

Aisle 1: peaches, spinach
Aisle 2: butter, cheese
Aisle 3: turkey, lamb

Before You Read [page 30]

b

Smart Supermarket Shopping

What did you read? [page 31]

a

Read again [page 31]

1. yes   2. yes   3. no   4. no   5. yes

Show you understand [page 31]

(Answers may vary)

Food	People	Money savers
fruit	checker	coupons
vegetables	packer	special sales
cereal	shopper	recycle cans
soup		store brands
apple		
sandwich		
bread		
pasta		
yogurt		
milk		

Before You Read [page 33]

1. a   2. b

Read for Your Health!

Read again [page 34]

Papa's	Maria's
X	
	X
	X
X	

Scan for numbers [page 34]

1. 448 calories; 330 calories
2. 21 g. fat; 13 g. fat
3. 1,115 mg. sodium; 500 mg. sodium

Unit 6

Before You Read [page 36]

1. b   2. b

Norma's Restaurant Review

What did you read? [page 37]

a

Read again [page 37]

1. b   2. a   3. a   4. b   5. a   6. b

Show you understand [page 37]

(Answers may vary)

People	Food	On the table
waitress	scrambled eggs	place mats
busboy	toast	napkins
cashier	pancakes	silverware
customer	sausage	glass
	onions	fork
	peppers	
	potatoes	
	cheese	

Words, words, words [page 38]

1. a   2. a   3. b   4. a   5. b

Word Forms: plurals with –s and –es [page 38]

Singular	Plural
waitress	waitresses
glass	glasses
potato	potatoes
busboy	busboys
cup	cups
onion	onions

Before You Read [page 39]

1. a   2. a

Breakfast at Nat's

Read again [page 40]

1. yes   2. yes   3. no   4. yes   5. yes

Show you understand [page 40]

Guest Check #1		Guest Check #2	
$5.25			$4.50
$6.00			$2.00
$1.25			$1.50
$1.25			$5.00
Total	$13.75		$2.50
		Total	$15.50

Unit 7

Art Student to Fashion Designer

Before You Read [page 42]

X sew   X design   X outfit   X shoes

What did you read? [page 43]

A fashion designer begins her career.

Read again [page 43]

1. She likes to **draw** and **sew**.
2. She meets the **manager** of a big **department store**.
3. She makes **five outfits**.
4. ...**shoes, purses, wallets, watches, eyeglasses, gloves, umbrellas**

Show you understand [page 43]

2 Cynthia listens to her roommate's idea...
5 Cynthia becomes a famous fashion designer.
1 Cynthia Rowley goes to art school.
4 Cynthia brings her clothes...
3 Cynthia meets a department store manager...

Words, words, words [page 44]

1. a   2. b   3. a   4. b

Free Work Clothes

Before You Read [page 45]

a

What did you read? [page 46]

a

Read again [page 46]

1. a   2. b   3. a   4. b   5. b

Words, words, words [page 46]

(Answers may vary.)

Clothes for men	ties
Clothes for women	dresses, skirts, blouses
Clothes for both	suits, pants, shirts, uniforms, shoes

Unit 8

Talk About It [page 47]

1. pharmacy
2. doctor's office
3. hospital

The Barter Clinic

Before You Read [page 48]

1. c   2. b

What did you read? [page 49]

b

Read again [page 49]

1. no   2. yes   3. yes   4. no   5. yes

Show you understand [page 49]

1. X   2. X   5. X   6. X

Words, words, words [page 50]

1. b   2. a   3. b   4. b   5. b

What Doctors Ask

Before You Read [page 51]

X exercise
X medicine
X head
X problem
X high blood pressure
X stomach

What did you read? [page 52]

b

Read again [page 52]

1. b   2. a   3. e   4. d   5. c

Words, words, words [page 52]

1. shoulder
2. exercise
3. headache
4. coughing
5. medicine

Unit 9

Talk About It [page 53]

Answers may vary.

Before You Read [page 54]

1. a   2. b

A Trip on Route 66

What did you read? [page 56]

Keiko is taking an interesting trip on Route 66.

Read again [page 56]

1. no   2. yes   3. no   4. yes   5. yes

Show you understand [page 56]

Places on Route 66	Illinois	Texas	Arizona	California
Chicago	X			
Standin' on the Corner Park			X	
The Midpoint Cafe		X		
Los Angeles				X
Winslow			X	

Scan for numbers [page 57]

1. 2,400   2. 8   3. 1926
4. 1970   5. 150   6. 12

Neighbor to Neighbor

What did you read? [page 60]

b

Read again [page 60]

1. b   2. b   3. a   4. a   5. a

Show you understand [page 60]

1. c   2. a   3. d   4. e   5. b

Unit 10

Before You Read [page 62]

1. a   2. b

Get Behind the Wheel

What did you read? [page 63]

b

Read again [page 63]

X 2. You put your key in the ignition. Then you put on your seat belt.

X 4. You drive with one hand on the steering wheel.

X 6. You signal after you change lanes.

Show you understand [page 63]

	Before …	At …	After …
Bring your …		X	
Be on time.		X	
Put gas …	X		
Shake hands …			X
Check the …	X		
Get your …			X

Words, words, words [page 64]

1. windshield wipers   4. headlights
2. tires   5. ignition
3. horn   6. signal

Puzzle: Mixed-up bumper stickers [page 64]

1. HOW IS MY DRIVING? CALL 555-8265.
2. ARE YOU READING THIS? YOU ARE TOO CLOSE!
3. ALWAYS WEAR YOUR SEAT BELT

Before You Read [page 65]

1. a   2. b

Jeff's First Driving Lesson

Read again [page 66]

1. yes   2. no   3. yes   4. yes   5. no   6. no

Show you understand [page 66]

… He puts on his **seat belt**. His friend Dana says, Now put your foot on the **gas pedal**. Soon they come to an **intersection**. Jeff stops the car and turns the **steering wheel** to the right. …Dana shouts, "Stop the car! Put your foot on the **brake**."

Unit 11

The Pennsylvania Macaroni Company

Before You Read [page 68]

1. b   2. a

What did you read? [page 70]

a

Read again [page 70]

1. They are from **Italy**.
2. They start a **pasta factory**.
3. Their business is in **Pittsburgh**.
4. There is a big **fire**.
5. It sells **pasta**, **cheese**, and **olive oil**.

Show you understand [page 70]

3 The Sunseri factory burns in a fire.

1 Augustino, Salvatore and Michael Sunseri come to the United States.

5 Jimmy and Nino Sunseri are working at the family business.

2 The three Sunseri brothers start a pasta factory.

4 Augustino Sunseri's sons start selling olive oil and cheese.

Words, words, words [page 71]

1. b   2. a   3. a   4. a   5. a

Working Moms

Before You Read [page 72]

1. a   2. b

Read again [page 74]

1. b   2. a   3. a   4. b   5. a

Unit 12

Before You Read [page 76]

1. a   2. b

No Snow? No Problem!

What did you read? [page 77]

b

Read again [page 77]

1. The main activity is **skiing**.

2. There are **30** snowdomes.

3. It costs about **$50** for the day.

4. There are **no** snowdomes in the United States now.

Show you understand [page 77]

In a snowdome, people can go **skiing** in the summer. Snowdomes have **snow** inside. People can ski **indoors**. Skiing isn't the only activity in a snowdome. Some snowdomes have **swimming pools**. It costs about $50 to go skiing in a snow dome. People can see about five **movies** for the same price!

Words forms [page 78]

Base form	*-ing* form
swim	swimming
run	running
climb	climbing
play	playing
ski	skiing
plan	planning

Before You Read [page 79]

X Thanksgiving

X Valentine's Day

X Memorial Day

X Fourth of July

Fit for the Holidays

What did you read? [page 80]

b

Read again [page 80]

1. yes   2. no   3. no   4. yes

Show you understand [page 80]

1. X   2. X   4. X   5. X

WORD LIST

Here are the words from *Read All About It Starter* that are in *The Basic Oxford Picture Dictionary*. To find a word in this list, look for the title of the reading where you saw the word, and then find the word under the title. The first number after each word refers to the page in *The Basic Oxford Picture Dictionary* where you can find the word. The second number (or letter) refers to the item on that page.

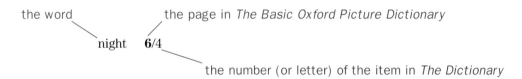

If only the **bold** page number appears, that word is part of the unit title or subtitle or somewhere else on the page.

The words in the list are in the form you see in the reading. When the word in the list has a very different form from the word in the *Dictionary*, you will see the *Dictionary* word next to it (babies   baby   **11**/1). When the word in the reading is used as a different part of speech from that of the word in the *Dictionary*, the part of speech appears after the word in the list.

n. = noun; v. = verb; adv.= adverb; *adj.*= adjective

Words in the list that are in **bold** type are verbs or verb phrases.

Unit 1 Weather Watch

How's the Weather?, page 3

around   **79**/10
blue   **9**/7
changing   **29**/L
circle   **9**/1
cloudy   **8**/5
coats   **50**/11
day   **5**/14
fall   **4**/16
farmers   **85**/20
fishermen   fisherman   **85**/18
gray   **9**/11
heavy   **52**/1
learn   **15**/L
listen   **15**/L
look at   **3**/H
moon   **6**/6
morning   **6**/1
night   **6**/4
old   **13**/24,

people   **11**
rain *n.*   **8**/1
rainy *adj.*   **8**/1
red   **9**/6
sleeping   (see **go to sleep**)   **15**/P
snow *n.*   **8**/2
stars   **6**/7
sun   **6**/5
sunny   **8**/4
talks   **3**/L
television   **24**/14
today   **5**/12
tomorrow   **5**/13
watch   **93**/K
weather   **8**
white   **9**/5
winter   **4**/13

The Groundhog Weather Report, page 7

below   **54**/2
brown   **9**/10
cloudy   **8**/5

cold **8**/12
day **5**/14
eat **15**/I
fall **4**/16
February **4**/2
freezing **8**/13
green **9**/9
into **79**/8
leaves **81**/B
morning **6**/1
north **97**/15
people **11**
sleep (see **go to sleep**) **15**/P
small **12**/8
snow *n.* **8**/2
spring **4**/14
summer **4**/15
sunny **8**/4
temperature **8**/8
under **54**/9
wakes up **14**/A
warm **8**/10
weather **8**
weeks **5**/15
winter **4**/13

Unit 2 Up and Down Days

Life Above Ground, page 11

above **54**/1
afternoon **6**/2
around **79**/10
breakfast **15**/I
bring **91**/A
California **98**
cell phone (tele)phone **24**/7
child **11**/6
climbs **87**/I
clothes **48**/53
cold **8**/12
cooks **15**/N
cut down *v.* (see **cut grass**) **88**/F
day **5**/14
exercises **64**/F
face **58**/I
friends **95**/0
gets dressed **14**/H
hair **13**
home **15**/M
learn **15**/L

letters **71**/5
life **20–21**
mail **89**/R
man **11**/5
morning **6**/1
over **78**/1
people **11**
reads **3**/E
scared **18**/6
sleep (see **go to sleep**) **15**/P
snows **8**/2
talk **3**/L
tall **12**/1
today **5**/12
tree (see **plant a tree**) **29**/Q
washes **wash** **14**/E
water **43**/4
week **5**/15
windy **8**/3
winter **4**/13
woman **11**/4
working **15**/K
young **13**/22

Life Below Ground, page 15

bed **26**/7
breakfast **15**/I
closes **3**/I
closing *adj.* **close** **3**/I
coffee **38**/11
conductor **85**/23
cup **42**/7, **101**
day **5**/14
dinner **15**/N
doors **22**/4
drives (see **drive a taxi**) **89**/O
eat **15**/I
get dressed **14**/H
go to bed **15**/0
hand **58**/5
home **15**/M
house **15**/J
leaves **81**/B
life **20–21**
man **11**/5
middle-aged **13**/23
opens **3**/J
passengers **80**/1
school **68**/1
stand **3**/N

starts   (see **start school**)   20/B
stop   73/D
stop   (see bus stop)   **72**/11
street   73/E
subway   **76**/7
take a shower   14/C
time   **4–7**
train   **76**/9
wake up   14/A
watch   93/K
work   15/K

Unit 3 HiTech Families

Teresa's Web Page, page 18

babies   baby   **11**/1
brother   **16**/5
excited   **18**/7
family   **16**
father   **16**/2
friends   **95**/0
graduated   20/C
homesick   **19**/14
job   **20**/D
July   **4**/7
June   **4**/6
look at   3/H
mother   **16**/3
moving   21/J
music   **93**/L
nervous   **18**/4
new   **52**/3
party   **17**
pictures   (see **take a picture**)   17/G
scared   **18**/6
school   **68**/I
September   **4**/9
sister   **16**/4
teachers   **2**/4
time   **4–7**
tired   **19**/10
today   **5**/12
worried   **19**/9

Computer Talk, page 21

birthday   (see birthday party)   **17**
cards   **17**/J
computer   **2**/13
day   **5**/14
family   **16**

friends   **95**/0
homesick   **19**/14
jobs   **20**/D
learn   15/L
letters   **71**/5
little   **12**/8
money   **10**
pen   **2**/10
people   **11**
presents   (see **give a present**)   17/A
reporter   **86**/7
scared   **18**/6
send   95/R
talk   3/L
telephone   **24**/7
time   **4–7**
today   **5**/12
week   **5**/15
work   15/K,
write   3/A

Unit 4 Homes on the Edge

A Yurt: A Home to Go, page 24

build   88
cloth   **30**/5
deck   **22**/10
door   **22**/4
floor   **24**/3
friends   **95**/0
front   (see front door) **78**/3
hammer   **31**/4
heavy   **52**/1
home   (see **come home**) 15/M
large   **12**/7
measure   87/G
move   21/J
nails   **31**/15
over   **78**/1
people   **11**
put in   87/B
roof   **22**/2
size   **12**
tape measure   **31**/7
time   **4–7**
today   **5**/12
tools   **31**
walls   **24**/2
windows   **22**/5
world   **96–97**

At Home on a Houseboat, page 27

activities   **92–93**
appliances   **88**/A
bathroom   **27**
bedrooms   **26**
bookcases   **24**/12
carpet   **26**/6
children   child   **11**/6
closets   **26**/1
collection *n.*   (see **collect garbage**)   **89**/U
community   **68–69**
driveway   **22**/7
freezer   **25**/15
garbage   **89**/U, **28**/J
home   **15**/M
kitchen   **25**
large   **12**/7
living room   **24**
microwave   **25**/1
new   **52**/3
oven   **25**/7
refrigerator   **25**/16
shower   (see **take a shower**)   **27**/1
sink   **27**/7
stove   **25**/6
time   **4–7**
today   **5**/12
toilet   **27**/12

Unit 5 Shop Smart

Smart Supermarket Shopping, page 30

aisles   **40**/2
apple   **35**/3
around   **79**/10
bags   **40**/11
bottles   **90**/4
bread   **38**/9
buy   **73**/G
cans   **37**/8
carton   **37**/1
cash register   **40**/8
cereal   **38**/10
checker   **40**/6
checkout   **40**/9
choose   **41**/D
customer   **40**/5
eat   **95**/Q
fish   **36**/10
foods   **44–45**

groceries   **40**/10
home   (see **come home**)   **15**/M
hungry   **19**/11
look   **3**/H
milk   **38**/1
money   **10**
morning   **6**/1
packer   **41**/12
pasta   **39**/17
people   **11**
salad   **45**/14
sandwich   **44**/10
shelves   shelf   **40**/1
shop *v.*   (see shopping cart)   **40**/4
shopping cart   **40**/4
soup   **39**/18
supermarket   **40**/41
time   **4–7**
today   **5**/12
walk   **73**/I
yogurt   **38**/8

Read for Your Health!, page 33

cheese   **38**/5
eat   **15**/I
fat   **12**/4
flour   **38**/13
food   **34–39**
garlic   **34**/6
healthy *adj.*   (see Health Care)   **65**
ingredients   **47**/K
love   **21**/F
low   **52**/8
mushrooms   **34**/14
oil   **38**/14
onions   **34**/12
pizza   **45**/16
reading *n.*   **read**   **3**/E
salt   **39**/22
sausage   **44**/2
size   **12**
slice *n.*   **46**/D
spinach   **34**/4
sugar   **38**/3
tomatoes   tomato   **34**/8
water   **43**/4

Unit 6 Let's Eat Out

Norma's Restaurant Review, page 36

arrives   **81**/D
around   **79**/10
booth   **43**/3
breakfast   **15**/I
brings   **91**/A
busboy   **43**/5
cashier   **43**/12
cheese   **38**/5
coffee   **38**/11
counter   **25**/14
cup   **42**/7
customers   **40**/5
describe   **52–53**
eat   **15**/I
eggs   **38**/4
food   **34–39**
fork   **42**/11
glass   **42**/6
juice   **39**/20
large   **12**/7
look at   **3**/H
meal   **46–47**
menu   **43**/8
napkins   **42**/10
onions   **34**/12
orange   **35**/4
pancakes   **44**/7
peppers   **34**/9
pick up   **91**/K
potatoes   potato   **34**/11
restaurant   **43**
sausage   **44**/2
scrambled eggs   **44**/1
syrup   **44**/8
table   **42**/1
toast   **44**/4
today   **5**/12
waitress   **43**/7
water   **43**/4

Breakfast at Nat's, page 39

apple   **35**/3
bacon   **36**/5
bake   **47**/L
breakfast   **15**/I
cheese   **38**/5
coffee   **38**/11
day   **5**/14

eggs   **38**/4
grapefruit   **35**/6
green   **9**/0
ham   **36**/6
juice   **39**/20
large   **12**/7
menu   **43**/8
milk   **38**/1
muffin   **44**/5
onion   **34**/12
orange   **35**/4
pancakes   **44**/7
pepper   **39**/23
restaurant   **43**
sausage   **44**/2
scrambled eggs   **44**/1
small   **12**/8
syrup   **44**/8
tea   **38**/12
toast   **44**/4
tomato   **34**/8

Unit 7 Working Clothes

Art Student to Fashion Designer, page 42

clothes   **48–53**
day   **5**/14
department store   **69**/20
glasses   **55**/8
gloves   **50**/13
men   man   **11**/5
Monday   **5**/2
morning   **6**/1
needles   **57**/1
new   **52**/3
New York   **99**
purses   **55**/5
sew   **57**/A
sewing machine   **57**/7
shoes   **48**/8
stops   **72**/D
student   **2**/5
thread   **57**/2
train   **76**/9
umbrellas   **50**/9
wallets   **55**/9
watches   watch   **55**/6
wears   **95**/M
women   woman   **11**/4
works   **15**/K

Free Work Clothes, page 45

blouses **48**/2
clothes **48–53**
dresses **48**/1
extra-large **53**/20
job (see **get a job**) **20**/D
large **53**/19
medical **66–67**
money **10**
Ohio **99**
pants **48**/7
shirts **48**/4
shoes **48**/8
sizes **12**
skirts **48**/3
small **53**/17
suits **48**/9
ties **48**/5
uniforms **48**/11
white **9**/5
work **88–89**

Unit 8 Call the Doctor!

The Barter Clinic, page 48

coat **50**/11
day **5**/14
doctor **66**/6
eggs **38**/4
examines **67**/F
fruit **35**
gives shots **67**/I
happy **18**/2
meet **81**/E
money **10**
name (see **print name**) **67/B**
office **83**/16
paint **87**/K
patients **66**/5
pay (see **pay for**) **41**/C
prescriptions **66**/10
repair **88**
shots (see **give a shot**) **64**/4
vegetables **34**
waiting room **66**/1
wears **95**/M
white **9**/5
work **88–89**
writes a prescription **67**/J

What Doctors Ask, page 51

blood pressure **63**/13
coughing *n.* **cough** **63**/B
doctor **66**/6
exercise **64**/F
feel *v.* (see feelings) **18–19**
headache **62**/3
health (see Health Care) **65**
heating pad **65**/6
high blood pressure **63**/13
medicines **64**/1
nervous **18**/4
office **83**/16
shoulder **58**/3
sore throat **63**/12
stomach **59**/27
taking medicine **64**/D

Unit 9 Community Spirit

A Trip on Route 66, page 55

apple pie **45**/22 (see also apple) **35**/3
April **4**/4
Arizona **98**
bakery **68**/10
bench **72**/12
between **54**/4
bigger big **12**/7
bus **76**/2
California **98**
corner **72**/5
crosses **cross** **73**/E
died **21**/L
excited **18**/7
family **16**
friends **95**/O
long **53**/13
mail **73**/F
name (see **print name**) **67/B**
opened **17**/J
package **71**/2
park **68**/7
people **11**
pie **45**/22
shirt **48**/4
sidewalk **72**/9
small **12**/8
stopped **73**/D
Texas **98**
waiting **67**/E

Unit 11 Working Families

A Business with a History, page 69

big **12**/7
brothers **16**/5
build **88**
businessmen businessman **86**/8
cheese **38**/5
deliver **89**
factory *n.* (see factory workers) **85**/13
factory workers **85**/13
families family **16**
fire **74**/2
food **34–39**
market **83**/18
morning **6**/1
new **52**/3
oil **38**/14
open **17**/J, **3**/J
oversee **87**/D
pasta **39**/17
Pennsylvania **99**
pounds **101**
put in **41**/E
restaurants **43**
sad **18**/3
sell **88**
short **12**/3
sons **6**/12
supermarkets **40**/41
today **5**/12
truck drivers **85**/19
trucks **76**/3
United States **98–99**
week **5**/15
work **88–89**
working **15**/K

Working Moms. page 73

computer **2**/13
computer programmer **86**/4
daughter **16**/13
day-care (see day-care center) **90–91**
families family **16**
home (see **come home**) **15**/M
husband **16**/9
job (see **get a job**) **20**/D
leaving *n.* **leave** **81**/B
money **10**
mothers **16**/3

office **83**/16
people **11**
talk **3**/L
work **15**/K
working *adj.* **15**/K

Unit 12 Keeping Fit

No Snow? No Problem!, page 76

activities activity **92–93**
basketball (see **play basketball**) **92**/E
big **12**/7
cold **8**/12
day **5**/14
days **5**/14
hot **8**/9
movies (see **go to the movies**) **93**/J
play **91**/C
pools (see **take care of pools**) **89**/M
rock-climbing (see **climb**) **87**/I
ski (see **go skiing**) **92**/H
skiing *n.* (see **go skiing**) **92**/H
snow *n.* **8**/2
sport **92**
spring **4**/14
summer **4**/15
swimming (see **go swimming**) **93**/M
United States **98–99**
walls **24**/2
warm **8**/10
weather **8**
winter **4**/13
world **96–97**

Fit for the Holidays, page 79

basketball (see **play basketball**) **92**/E
big **12**/7
community **68–69**
cookies **39**/21
day **5**/14
exercise *n.* **64**/F
fireworks (see **watch fireworks**) **95**/K
Fourth of July) **95**
go running **93**/N
holiday **94–95**
January **4**/1
July **4**/7
learn **15**/L
look **3**/H
meal **46–47**

REMEMBER THE WORDS

Learn new words. Follow the steps to fill in the chart. Study the chart, and you will soon remember the words.

1. Choose a word you want to remember and write it in the chart.

2. Find out how to say the word and write it in a way you can remember. Ask an English-speaking friend, look in a dictionary, or ask your teacher.

3. Find out what it means and write the meaning. Look in the reading for clues. Ask your partner, classmate, family member, or an English-speaking friend. Look in a dictionary or ask your teacher.

4. Copy the sentence from the reading.

UNIT	1. WHAT IS THE WORD?	2. HOW DO YOU SAY IT?	3. WHAT DOES IT MEAN?	4. SENTENCE FROM THE READING
1	cows	kauz	animals, they give milk.	The cows are sleeping.

©2005 Oxford University Press
Permission granted to reproduce for classroom use.

UNIT	1. WHAT IS THE WORD?	2. HOW DO YOU SAY IT?	3. WHAT DOES IT MEAN?	4. SENTENCE FROM THE READING

©2005 Oxford University Press
Permission granted to reproduce for classroom use.

UNIT	1. WHAT IS THE WORD?	2. HOW DO YOU SAY IT?	3. WHAT DOES IT MEAN?	4. SENTENCE FROM THE READING

©2005 Oxford University Press
Permission granted to reproduce for classroom use.